Essays in Ethnographic Theory

The ethnographic essay provides a creative form for new work in anthropology. Longer than a journal article, shorter than a conventional monograph, ethnographic essays are experiments in anthropological thought, probing particular cases, topics, or arguments, to propose in-depth but concentrated analyses with unusual insight. In the past these were often published by research institutes or academic departments, but in recent years the style has enjoyed less space than it deserves. Hau Books is pleased to offer room for renewing the essay as an anthropological genre. Our Essays in Ethnographic Theory are published as short books, in print, and as open-access PDF editions.

T0049137

The Immensity of Being Singular

Approaching Migrant Lives in São Paulo through Resonance

HAU
Books

Director
Anne-Christine Taylor

Editorial Collective
Deborah Durham
Catherine V. Howard
Nora Scott
Hylton White

Managing Editor
Jane Sabherwal

HAU Books are published by the
Society for Ethnographic Theory (SET)

www.haubooks.org

The Immensity of Being Singular

Approaching Migrant Lives in São Paulo through Resonance

Simone Toji

HAU Books

Chicago

Cover design: Ania Zayco and Daniele Meucci
Layout design: Deepak Sharma, Prepress Plus
Typesetting: Prepress Plus (www.prepressplus.in)

ISBN: 978-1-912808-57-1 [paperback]
ISBN: 978-1-912808-77-9 [PDF]
LCCN: 2021931417

Hau Books
Chicago Distribution Center
11030 S. Langley Ave.
Chicago, Il 60628
www.haubooks.org

Hau Books publications are printed, marketed, and distributed
by The University of Chicago Press.
www.press.uchicago.edu

Printed in the United States of America on acid-free paper.

To Maria and Masaaki

Contents

Contents

Acknowledgments

My debt of gratitude goes to those who became my interlocutors during my fieldwork from September 2013
to January 2015 in the city of São Paulo and were generous in sharing their experiences. Although I can only
name them by pseudonyms, I am immensely grateful to
Kitty, Mr. Kwon, Julieta, Helen and Liu. Some of them
were not initially identified as research participants, but
when I asked permission to use data related to them and
our experiences together, they generously agreed, trusting the care and respect I dedicated to each of them in
the different relationships we developed. With them, I
engaged with a diverse array of involvements and commitments: I enrolled myself in sewing classes as the garment industry was the economic engine of Bom Retiro,
the area of my study; I became an employee at a local
flower shop and a restaurant; I volunteered at a migrant
women's social movement; I taught basic Portuguese for
non-Brazilians at a public school in the neighborhood;
I translated during regular visits to the local health
unit; and I also had the opportunity to travel to Bolivia. Fieldnotes, interviews, Portuguese exercises, and
conversations during medical appointments became

materials for the making of this ethnographic project. This book is an effort to live up to the trust invested by Kitty, Mr. Kwon, Julieta, Helen and Liu in my research work.

A wholehearted acknowledgement goes to Nigel Rapport. As my doctoral supervisor at the time I was writing up my thesis, he was the one to see the potentialities of my project. For his attentive support and daring provocations, I am forever thankful. He was the one to understand the "messiness" I brought with my research preoccupations, because when he first returned from the field he impressed upon his doctoral supervisor that he wanted to write about the complexity and inconsistency of things: "Social life was not about neat, mechanical models, about overarching systems, whatever may be the conventional wisdom about structure and function, synthesis and consensus. Social life was farcical, chaotic, multiple, contradictory; it was a muddling-through" (Rapport 1993: ix). Working with me, it was his turn to be "impressed upon" . . .

This book is largely based on the research undertaken for my doctoral thesis, presented at the University of St Andrews in 2016. However, during the preparation of this book, I had the chance to revisit fieldwork notes, relocate passages and reframe questions to sharpen the arguments and make the text more enjoyable. The research was made possible thanks to funding from the CAPES Foundation within the Ministry of Education of Brazil, which supported my doctoral studies and part of my field work.

The Instituto do Patrimônio Histórico e Artístico Nacional (IPHAN) provided me with the time to develop these studies by granting a leave of study from September 2012 to November 2016. My interest in understanding the lives of international migrants in the neighborhood of Bom Retiro was sparked by a cultural heritage project I coordinated at this organization.

Much has evolved since I proposed to publish the core outcomes of my doctoral studies as a book. For this, I have to absolutely thank Hylton White and Nanette Norris, at HAU Books, for their invaluable patience and backing during the whole publishing process, as much as their belief in my proposal. Likewise, I owe a great deal to the three anonymous reviewers whose comments pushed me to make this book more organic and alive. Also, to Matthew Wilhelm-Solomon, who helped me to hone the words and the writing styles to best convey the experimental exercise I am proposing here. It was a pleasure and an honor to work with him.

I am also grateful to Michele Wisdahl, *in memoriam*, for her comments on parts of the text, to Lisa Keating for her assistance in making the manuscript more accurate, and to Fernando for his care and love. Certainly, all shortcomings are exclusively mine.

Wonderings

One morning in February 2014, Kitty confided to me that she was pregnant and that she did not know what to do. She had messaged me the day before; she was apprehensive about her new situation and wanted to meet. When we met at a community center in the neighborhood of Bom Retiro, she started our conversation by saying, "my life is a mess, my life is a complete mess!" She was profoundly disappointed that, after learning of her pregnancy, Jimmy—her boyfriend at the time—did not take responsibility. Instead, Jimmy told her that he was seeing another girl and did not know what to do either. Both of them were in their twenties and had recently arrived from Paraguay to live and work in São Paulo. Kitty questioned Jimmy about money to buy abortion pills, but he replied that he had spent all of it on mobile phone credit and food.

Although Jimmy's answers might sound insensitive to an unsuspecting bystander, they indicated how precarious his life as a migrant was in São Paulo. I warned Kitty that abortion was not legal in Brazil and, in most cases, would be considered a criminal offense. She would have no support from the local health system and should carefully consider her options before deciding to terminate the pregnancy. If she decided to have the baby, the public health system in São Paulo would assist her, even in the case that she did not hold the documents for legal residence in the country. Kitty listened to me silently and when I asked her what she would like to do, she faltered, lowered her eyes, and sighed, "I don't know, I don't know . . ."

Disarmed by Kitty's hesitancy and confusion, I realized at that very instant how easily a person's existence can be completely disrupted. There are times when things do not happen exactly as we expect and the inconstancy of life demands the entire reformulation of our worlds. For Kitty, that moment required the difficult decision between having a child, probably without a father, or risking her life with an illegal abortion in Brazil. Neither choice pointed to an easy resolution.

If Kitty's circumstances showed, in drastic terms, how unsettling people's lives can be, other international migrants I encountered in the city of São Paulo also enhanced my awareness that uncertainty and inconstancy are constituents of life itself.

On a warm afternoon in January 2015, I visited Julieta at her house in the neighboring municipality of Cotia. On this occasion, she invited me to sit on the veranda to enjoy the freshness of the garden. Julieta confessed that she loved to spend her weekends with her husband and their kids in that garden. The projections for her husband's store equipment business were not altogether positive. She also worked there as a sales administrator but she did not have much to complain about. When they were short of money, they took pleasure in merely being together in the garden, playing with the children and the dogs. That was a simple joy that she did not imagine would be so precious. She was not sure about their future. Maybe they would sell the house and join her parents in Quillacollo, Bolivia. Julieta did not know exactly how their lives would be in the coming years, but that was not a pressing problem. She grinned and added, in her usual affectionate manner, that if they moved to Bolivia, I would always have a place to stay there. Although Julieta's situation did not convey the urgency of Kitty's, uncertainty and instability also impacted the course of her life. In Julieta's case, her acceptance that unpredictability was a natural factor in the art of making plans gave her a calm attitude concerning family projects.

What caught my attention in the migrants' stories that I followed in São Paulo was the fact that life itself could be deemed a "mess," as Kitty stated so desperately. Life was never certain: it was a constant striving and a continual source of concern. Moments of indecision and suspension emerged as part and parcel of these individuals' life processes.

Challenged by the "messiness" embedded in the lives of some international migrants in the city of São Paulo, this book is an effort to recognize "messiness" as an integral element of life processes. It is an invitation to consider ethnography as a form of appreciation of the contradictions and ambiguities involved in the making of life itself. Through documenting the lives of the migrants I came to know, I found that ethnicity or nationality need to be displaced as central references for understanding their condition. Categories of ethnicity and nationality were not sufficient to conceptualize the variability of experiences at stake without losing the richness involved in each migrant's particular effort to make life possible. As a consequence, this book is also a critique of categorization and generalization as productive operations in ethnography and in migration studies.

Without giving proper attention to the singular ways in which each person comes to exist in the world, we miss the opportunity to explore people's unique power to invent and reinvent their lives—a significant aspect of the human condition. For—as I intend to show—no life is lived in general terms.

Messiness

Uncontrolled human or non-human phenomena such as financial crises, pandemics, or environmental disasters are nowadays recurrently affecting our routines. More and more, scholarship has been consolidating risk, uncertainty, and precarity as key words of the contemporary age. While Ulrich Beck (1992, 2009) considers risk the central standard in our present societies for a new range of transformations based on uncertainty, Anna Tsing (2015) argues that precarity has become the condition of our time because indeterminacy is making us increasingly vulnerable. Concurrently, precarity has also been identified as the predominant facet of work and life in a world that shifted from stable and regular modes of production toward flexible regimes (Harvey 1990, 2012; Lash and Urry 1988, 1994; Standing 2011; Allison 2013; Davis 2006).

The "messiness" composing the experiences of the mobile subjects in this ethnography expresses the processes outlined in these debates. However, the contribution of this book lies in understanding the uncertainty and instability associated with this messiness, not as elements of a specific historical conjuncture, but as existential constituents of the process of life-making itself. In this way, the messiness found in the daily routines of a few migrants in the metropolitan area of São

Paulo requires considering a more general horizon of the human condition. This comprehension stands close to what Judith Butler (2004, 2010) named "precariousness": a common human condition of being fragile. Such fragility refers to the fact that no human life has its existence in the world guaranteed. As human beings, we are exposed to all sorts of misfortune and, in being vulnerable in this manner, we inevitably become dependent on our responsibility to recognize and regard one another's presences.

Furthermore, distinguishing "precariousness" and "precarity," Butler defines precarity as the effects of the unequal distribution of economic, political, and social assets that disenfranchise subjects in our present time. These subjects are exposed to economic insecurity, injury, and violence; neoliberalism, war, and climate crises can aggravate the fragility of their beings. By differentiating precariousness from precarity, Butler allows us to separate a constructive and humane notion of precariousness from the disparaging meaning frequently attached to precarity. Though she keeps both concepts to analyze the unequal dynamics of our contemporary time, I concentrate on her concept of precariousness to support my exploration of messiness in the lives of international migrants in São Paulo. I do this to show that uncertainty and instability constitute, in an existential sense, the fragility of any human life.

Such a view on messiness can reveal its creative aspect in making life an open and constructive process, in which uncertainty and hesitation are fundamental factors for generating possibilities in a person's life course. As Tsing suggests, "indeterminacy also makes life possible" (2015: 20). In this book, my aim is to acknowledge uncertainty as an active component of existence, so that life can emerge as an ongoing effort to be in a world of ever-changing configurations. As a result, uncertainty can be embraced as a form of exploration that allows for the making of possibilities (Pink et al. 2018). These are mostly fleeting and fragile and never brought to consideration without a certain degree of concern or distress, as the lives to be portrayed in the coming chapters will show.

If the messiness identified in the course of the lives of those I met in São Paulo calls for the recognition of uncertainty and inconstancy as productive and defining aspects in the making of people's trajectories, it also requires awareness of the varied situations and often unexpected occurrences derived from it. Berthomé et al. (2012) assert that studying uncertainty requires attention to configurations emerging from the interactional dynamics produced by the participants—particular agents in a certain place and time create specific arrangements that cannot be found elsewhere. Nonetheless, these occurrences can be misapprehended when abstract systems of representations are unduly applied. This is the reason why uncertainty requires not only the attention to the particular and momentary in the world, but also appropriate theoretical and methodological approaches. Although pragmatism, as proposed by Berthomé et al., was not the approach applied to the cases I followed, the effort to find a way to theoretically and methodologically do justice to each life is shared by this book.

In his provocative work *After Method: Mess in Social Science Research,* John Law (2004) argues that, since the world is complex, fluid, and messy, research methods in social sciences cannot work exclusively on the assumption that realities are a set of determinate and identifiable processes. As "much of the world is vague, diffuse or unspecific, slippery, emotional, ephemeral, elusive or indistinct, and changes like a kaleidoscope" (Law 2004: 2), Law looks for ways of "pointing to and articulating a sense of the world as an unformed but generative flux of forces and relations that work to produce particular realities [...] [as] the world is not a structure, something we can map with our social science charts" (2004: 6–7). Accordingly, developing unusual and as yet unknown methods in social science may create room for these overlooked realities. Law encourages us to "imagine what research methods might be if they were adapted to a world that included and knew itself as tide, flux, and general unpredictability" (2004: 7). Therefore, to consider messiness as something integral to life processes and to the world we live in implies the need for conceiving new ways of thinking, doing research, and representing.

The messiness ingrained in the experiences shared with me in moments of confusion, uncertainty, or vagueness put into question the act of knowing as the sole achievement of a successful research endeavor. If the inconstancy of people's lives revealed how the world can be volatile and fluid, the unclear incidents I attempted to follow in the lives of some migrants also imparted the impression that there would be always a part of an event or a personal story that would not be disclosed. There was always this "mystery" in each person and in each occasion that prevented me from knowing them completely. This mystery was like an insistent reiteration that the closer one gets, the more distant one is. People continuously startled me with the renderings of their life trajectories. Every person was definitely a living surprise, a sort of open-ended manifestation, as I observed how each of them was able to engender unexpected solutions to certain life problems. People, in their peculiar ways of being-in-the-world, puzzled me profoundly. And to be open and receptive to these occurrences—as I sensed they were lived and articulated by my interlocutors—required a new research disposition.

This book was born out of the realization that, to explore what those who collaborated with me during fieldwork were recurrently raising with their experiences, I had to reconfigure the epistemological basis of my approach. In consequence, I also had to reconsider the means of identifying and describing such observations and tailor an ethnographic proposition more akin to what was being lived and ascertained. Thus, this account is simultaneously a proposal and an experiment.

The Imperfect Science

Malinowski (1932) established fieldwork as a foundational method in anthropology, seeking to guarantee a scientific standard for the discipline. In an influential chapter on method in *Argonauts of the Western Pacific*, Malinowski exhorted anthropologists to adopt practices for generalizing data and identifying patterns, such as the observation of "laws and regularities of cultural phenomena" (1932: 10), and the operations of "reducing information into charts and synoptic tables" (1932: 14). In doing so, anthropologists would be able to grasp the "skeleton of tribal constitution" (1932: 17), the essential forms that organized the existence of a social group. Yet Malinowski admitted that this schematization of people's lives would always lack "flesh and blood" (1932: 20), i.e., it would lack all the "small incidents" that constituted people's daily affairs. Whereas the "method of statistic documentation by concrete evidence" (1932: 17) aimed to find "the skeleton" of a specific society, the "small incidents" that constituted society's "flesh and blood" were considered as "imponderabilia of actual life" (1932: 20).

Although Malinowski considered the search for "laws and regularities" the scientific part of anthropology, he was aware that the "imponderabilia of actual life" was constituent of the anthropologist's observations as well. For him, the "imponderabilia of actual life" could not impart scientificity to the ethnographer's work, since its exponents were interest-led traders, missionaries, and officials of the colonial administration. However, "the imponderabilia of actual life" had always been admitted as part and parcel of anthropology, though not its most noble scientific component.

In my search for scientific references that are not based on uniformities and generalizations, Malinowski's "imponderabilia of actual life" inspired the ethnographic attitude of this book vis-à-vis the "messiness" shown in the lives I encountered. A consideration of "the imponderabilia of actual life" of some international migrants living in São Paulo will question the abstract logics of schematization and systematization as appropriate research operations, at the same time as it will propose to redeem the attention to details and particulars composing singular lives as a viable ethnographic approach. In line with what feminist scholarship has already encouraged, I push to the limits a sense of "situated knowledge" (Haraway 1991). I consider the qualifier "situated" as referring to the particularities that necessarily constitute our existences as singular beings establishing singular relationships in the world, and as an ethnographic practice that acknowledges those irreducible elements that constitute the very particularity of a life or a situation—which I will elaborate in the coming chapters as "methodological irreducibility." In order to do so, this investigation will join forces with the projects of a cosmopolitan (Rapport 2012a) and an existential anthropology (Jackson 2005). In the cosmopolitan project, an account of the human is only possible when based on the expression of the individual as a singular embodiment "that is not obscured or distorted by cultural prejudices, social structures or historical contingencies" (Rapport 2012a: 2). In an existential anthropology, the possibility of recognizing life as a "struggle for being"—and an experimentation in which people live the world in their own terms— is made available by not reducing existence to any one category, such as culture, mind, or nature (Jackson 2005: xii). By acknowledging people's presences as manifestations of an existential experimentation in the world, this ethnography attempts to reach an understanding of the human through the very singularity of the lives of some of the international migrants I encountered in the city of São Paulo.

A first move toward this proposition consists of granting to the aforementioned "mystery" within the lives I came across a heuristic quality for considering the human worlds to which I was exposed. It is in Levinas's (1987) notion of the irreducibility of the Other that I find recourse to express the insufficiency of any sort of systematization to do justice to the richness of people's lives, and the inspiration to engage with the mystery involved in the personal trajectories I was able to attend. Levinas believes that the "relationship with the Other is a relationship with a Mystery" (1987: 75); it is a recognition that the Other is not another myself. Despite the fact that I can recognize the Other as resembling me, the Other is an exteriority, an alterity that is unknowable to me. The Other is unreachable by categories of thought, because the act of gaining access to the Other through knowledge is not a relation with the Other, as the Other is thereby turned into an object referenced for a knowing subject. The Other is an exceeding, a mystery that overflows the thought that is being thought. Levinas (1967) calls this exceeding an "infinity". In acknowledging the absolute alterity of the Other, no totality is possible before the infinity produced in this relationship between the Other and me. This relationship cannot be reduced to understanding: it is an ethical relationship par excellence, in which I accept the insurmountable alterity of the Other, not by the assignment of a category of knowledge that encapsulates the Other, but by invoking the presence of the Other as a "face." The exteriority of the Other is actualized in our meeting in the world as "faces." The face of the Other is not a representation; it is already the manifestation of the relationship between me and the Other, in which both of us invoke one another as interlocutors.

Rapport (2015: 260) proposes an anthropology through Levinas in which the mystery of the Other is an opportunity to understand the "plurality of existence" not as a manifestation of a politics of identity, but as an aspiration for what is beyond holistic conceptualizations and I follow this path. In this regard, "respect for otherness is based on ignorance more than on knowledge: the relevance of ignorance is that it undermines not only myth and the conceptual and cultural but also the possibility of having other than an intimation of the absolute plurality of existence" (2015: 261).

As knowledge in a positivist sense is not the intended outcome of this research endeavor, this ethnographic experiment envisions itself as the manifestation of an ethical approach toward the people I encountered during fieldwork. By ethical approach, I mean the invocation of the presence of the people I met as "faces," in Levinas's terms. As faces, the people I met exceeded my ideas about them and could not be totally subsumed by overarching explanations. Not only were they a mystery, but each of them substantiated a singularity of their own through the many life moments they shared with me. So, the face of my interlocutors opened up in the mutual engagement we experienced together that I hereby refer to as "life-journeys." Each life-journey that emerged from the encounter with the face of the Other held a richness of its own as a continuous realization that life was not certain or easy. Life was in fact a constant experimentation that at times could not be deemed a coherent whole. In the openness of the life-journeys portrayed in the following chapters, a sense of "infinity" may sound exaggerated, but certainly these life-journeys could not be easily encompassed by senses of structural totality. As Levinas proposes, "the particular and the personal, which are unsurpassable, magnetize the very field in which the production of infinity is enacted" (1967: 26).

At this point, the imponderabilia of actual life reaches a broader significance. From the details and "small incidents" composing the non-scientific part of collective life, the imponderabilia moves to particulars that are irreducible to operations of totalization, particulars that lay claim to a different response from science: an ethical claim that the anthropologist be sensitive enough not to deface the Other in objectification.

In discovering possibility in Malinowski's and Levinas's considerations, this ethnographic endeavor aspires to elicit an anthropological approach that it is more an ethics—a considerate attendance to the presence of Others in the world—than a form of knowledge, an anthropological approach in which truth is not the outcome of a series of scientific procedures, but a form of appreciation of the human.

Mobile Trajectories in Brazil

The attention to the inconstancies of the migrants I had the chance to follow and to the specifics involved in each life-journey not only required a new ethnographic disposition but it also entailed a careful consideration regarding the question of categorization in migration studies. As such, the approach proposed here benefits from the analytical efforts already undertaken by studies exposing the disenfranchising effects of state and policy modes of classification that often disqualify migrants[1] as active agents with complex backdrops. In these acts of "labelling", migrants are then deemed to be refugees (Zetter 1991 and 2007; Sajjad 2018), forced or voluntary migrants (Erdal and Oeppen 2018), or economic migrants (Thiollet 2010). Central to the critical approach to labelling in the ethnographic approach I tailor here—ethically concerned with not reproducing inhumane measures of symbolic classification—is the concern with de-humanizing processes.

I thus interrogate a further facet of the preoccupation with labelling in migration studies, particularly those associated with categories of nationality and nation-state. In privileging the personal sense of each particular journey, the approach here blurs well-defined understandings of national boundaries or perceptions of belonging and follows Ulrich Beck's (2006) invitation to be wary of the methodological nationalism that may

---

1. I consider my interlocutors to be fundamentally international mobile actors. Although the term "migrant' may at times be loaded with varied assumptions, as mobility studies have already critiqued, I do not believe it is irrelevant for the cases I analyze. For this reason, I also refer to my interlocutors as international migrants.

be embedded in certain conventions of our research practices.

By being cautious about not imposing pre-conceived categories widely applied in migration studies, the ethnographic effort of this project stems from my interlocutors' ideas and viewpoints, appreciating them in their own terms. However, to gain a thicker perspective of their presences and comprehend the stakes of their specific positionalities, it is necessary to bear in mind the legacy that successive migration policies and movements have left by creating unequal standards that place migrants in asymmetrical positions within and beyond Brazilian society through the centuries.

It is not within the scope of the book to analyze the consecutive migration policies effected in Brazil, but it is important to pinpoint how they have continually sustained the production of difference and inequality. In a country with a colonial legacy in which the mass decimation of indigenous populations and slavery of African groups played a major role in the constitution of social, political, economic and cultural relations, migration policies were instrumental in maintaining certain disparities of the colonial period, a phenomenon Encarnación Gutiérrez Rodrígues (2018) called the "coloniality of migration." As an expression of this dynamic, in the nineteenth century, migration policies in Brazil were designed to inscribe varied degrees of alterity in a nation that was already divided about its African and indigenous heritages. Following other neighboring countries in Latin America that were interested in consolidating their positions as independent nation-states (Castles, de Haas and Miller 2014), Brazil also adopted migration policies as a means to "whiten" its national population (Seyferth 1996, Lesser 1999), inspired by evolutionist and racist theories and the desire to become

14

a "civilized" nation (Skidmore 1993, Schwarcz 1993). Throughout the nineteenth and the twentieth centuries, degrees of "whiteness" intersected with factors such as class, gender, religion, ethnicity and others, but in general the state's preferred migrant groups were those from European countries, where numerous regional or internal conflicts stimulated many to attempt a new life in settlements or plantations overseas. Migrants from Asian countries, though also admitted in analogous conditions, were considered "undesirable" (Ramos 1996, Dezem 2005). Later on, the Second World War rearranged such a frame, putting under suspicion nationals from Italy, Germany and Japan, given that Brazil supported the Allies.

By the end of the 1950s, processes of industrialization and urbanization changed the country's social and economic landscape and migration policies required skilled migrants that contributed to national manufacturing development. State concerns around economic development came to replace those about race, but the 1960s and 1970s saw a stark decline in international migrants entering the country in comparison to previous decades. Groups such as those from South Korea were the last ones sponsored by governmental initiatives (Choi 1991). In the 1980s, new migration configurations emerged, with Brazil also becoming a country of emigration (Margolis 2013, Feldman-Bianco 2001). In addition, the country was receiving increasing numbers of migrants from nations of the Global South, such as Bolivia, Peru, Paraguay, and China (Baeninger 2012).

Within Brazilian migration studies, from the 1930s to the 1970s, a period of consolidation of the social sciences in the country, migration processes were predominantly analysed as dynamics supporting the constitution of the Brazilian nation and revolved around concepts such as assimilation, integration and acculturation (De Oliveira 2018, Taniguti 2018). The new migratory dynamics of the 1980s onwards encouraged analyses about international migrants through the idea of the network (Truzzi 2008), since migratory movements turned out to be dependent on the multiple interconnections migrants arranged in order to relocate successfully. More recently, the presence of migrants coming from Africa (Baeninger and Peres 2011), Haiti (Patarra and Fernandes 2011) and Venezuela (De Oliveira 2019) are now prompting Brazilian scholars to explore ideas of refuge, asylum, and mixed migration (Silva et al. 2017).

Informed by this history and these studies, this ethnography approaches migrants by following Abdelmalek Sayad's insistence on asking "about the diversity of causes and reasons that may have determined the departures and oriented the diversity of trajectories" (2004:xiii). This book thus proposes to offer a detailed and vivid portrayal of international migrants' life-journeys, in a way that, as explained above, moves away from the act of labelling. Rather, the particular and the unexpected can be seen as constituent of their ordinary experience as individuals—originally born in South Korea, China, Paraguay or Bolivia—who had their lives reconfigured by their stay in Brazil.

São Paulo

São Paulo is a municipality of more than 12 million inhabitants, ranked among the ten richest and most populated cities in the world. Its population growth has decelerated in the last decades as the city is no longer a top destination for Brazilian nationals. Alongside this, it has been restructuring its economy and logistics, accumulating both industrial and high-valued service functions, and consolidating its position as a hub connected to production systems worldwide (Comin 2011). These changes also generated new "centralities" beyond the historical city center, sustaining new spatial references around Paulista and Juscelino Kubitchek Avenues (Frúgoli 2000). While central areas have been losing their significance in the overall urban dynamic, renovation initiatives in these zones has been couched in disputed processes of gentrification (Frúgoli and Sklair 2009).

A United Nations Human Settlements report referred to São Paulo as "a tale of two cities," in which poverty and violence engender appalling urban inequalities between its "center" and "peripheries" (UN-HABITAT 2010). As a divided city, São Paulo has also been defined as the expression of a misadjusted modernity that produced a problematic metropolis between the poles of "the archaic" and "the postmodern" (Maricato 1999). It is the result of private entrepreneurship in its central zone which pushed the urban poor to live in risky areas of the outskirts (Rolnik 1999). The city's geography is the product of an abysmal social and territorial segregation in which the different urban classes exist spatially and socially apart, with the upper-middle classes living in enclaves of gated condominiums while the lower classes subsist in precarious settlements near these enclosed complexes or in the suburbs (Caldeira 2000). Within this dichotomist framework, some studies have concentrated on one side of the divide, specifically on the peripheral and precarious areas like the "autoconstructed" lots (Holston 2009) or "slums" (Davies 2006). Likewise, other scholars also documented the divided city through the universe of the disenfranchised.

Attention to "urban populations" (Cardoso 1986) was then directed to the "excluded", either in the peripheries or the city center. In the peripheries, studies highlighted working-class groups organized around issues of urban infrastructure and housing (Bonduki and Rolnik 1979) and influence networks drawn along party political lines (Caldeira 1984). They also depicted particular practices of leisure (Magnani 1998) and claims to a periphery identity via hip-hop (Pardue 2010). In contrast, accounts regarding the city center detailed how this part of São Paulo was re-appropriated by workers from lower economic classes in precarious housing practices (Kowarick 2009) or by "unwanted" subjects, such as those struggling with crack addiction (Frúgoli and Spaggiari 2010; Rui 2014).

São Paulo, depicted in this way, is thus an unresolved, problematic and largely deficient urban space. By attending to international migrants' trajectories in the city, this ethnography views such a troubled urban space from a microscopic stance, understanding it as a place lived with different points of arrival and departure defined by the specifics of each life course. In proposing to observe a difficult city such as São Paulo through the lives I followed, I aim at appreciating a city with "faces," a city that is permeable to the ways each migrant traverses the city on their own terms, advancing distinct struggles. As a result, São Paulo has become connected to worldwide dynamics through the journeys of international migrants. Contradiction and ambiguity are part of these processes. As such, I want to explore the human capacities people develop for reinventing themselves in precarious and unequal urban environments, which São Paulo exemplifies. In this, I propose to view such an urban space as an existential experience deeply ingrained in people's everyday lives.

The Journey Ahead

This book is organized into five chapters, interweaving the theoretical arguments that made this ethnographic experiment possible with the personal trajectories I encountered in São Paulo. Chapter 1 presents the experimental approach through the researcher's imagination that is tailored to account for the fleeting and subtle aspects in the messy lives of the international migrants I met in the city of São Paulo. Imagination is used to make visible the unspoken incidents often overlooked by scholarly analyses. A phenomenological part of the methodology is then outlined in order to make manifest the limitations of the research endeavor before the inherent "mystery" I encountered, which is then acknowledged by the use of brief fictional narratives to evoke what was not completely identifiable, but present, in the lives of my interlocutors. Here we meet Kitty again to understand how my interlocutors come to be a "face" for this ethnographic experiment. Chapter 2 elaborates on how each trajectory becomes singular in its own unfolding process due to the imponderabilia of actual life. This time we accompany Helen and Mr. Kwon more closely to recognize the specificity of people's life courses. In Chapter 3, we go back to Kitty's trajectory in São Paulo in order to fully reach a comprehension of the singularity and openness of the trajectories being depicted here as "life-journeys." After outlining the core elements sustaining the ethnographic experiment being proposed, the life-journeys of Julieta and Liu are introduced in Chapter 4 to demonstrate how the approach underlines the transformative aspects of a person's experience. In Chapter 5, drawing on the richness of the particular life-journeys narrated in previous chapters, observations on migration and urban studies are derived from the experimental approach undertaken. In the final part of the book, I provide a summary of the attempted experiment and some of the insights gained through this exploration.

Resonance

I do not intend to speak about, just speak nearby.
Trinh Minh-ha, *Reassemblage*, 1982

The imponderabilia of the lives of the international mobile actors I encountered in São Paulo compelled me to develop a different ethnographic disposition, one that acknowledges the unattainability of fully knowing any being, privileging an ethical commitment towards the "faces" of my interlocutors. In this chapter, I elaborate on how this disposition also requires an associated effort to craft a kind of writing that articulates such concerns, by recognizing the partiality of our knowledge and, consequently, problematizing the assumptions of a realist genre. Following this insight, I compose an evocative style of ethnography. I venture on this path in the company of Kitty, who was already introduced above and taught me the significance of "being there" when nothing made sense.

Mystery and the Face of the Other

On the morning of March 31, 2014, I was escorting Kitty to her first medical appointment at the health unit in Bom Retiro. On our way, she mentioned that there were days when Jimmy stayed overnight with her. I asked if he was finally helping her with the pregnancy. She shook her head, commenting that the last time she saw him, he was drunk and arrived at her place about 5 a.m. Perplexed, I inquired why she allowed him to behave like that, without taking any responsibility or consideration towards her or the baby. Kitty became disconcerted and, shrugging her shoulders, groaned thoughtfully, "I don't know . . . you can't understand it." Indeed, I could not understand why she insisted on maintaining that painful relationship with Jimmy. However, I was embarrassed that my question sounded judgmental. At times, our research interlocutors urge us to respect situations that they likewise cannot fully understand. These moments stand beyond the researcher's scope of moral and research certainties; however, as fellow humans, we are called to recognize what we do not fully understand as a valid experience of being-in-the-world. I find in Levinas's notion of the unattainability of the Other an opportunity to elaborate further on such an ethical concern.

For Levinas (1967), the Other is a metaphysical reference, irreducible to any thought I may try to apply in order to capture them. The Other overwhelms me by all means and appears to me simply as a "face." The Other is unreachable and their face is an appearance in the phenomenal order that goes beyond plastic forms, because the face is not a representation of the Other. A face is not a physical face, it is the presence of alterity, the evocation of the proximity between me and the Other, a culmination of the ethical relationship that is instigated when "the face summons me, calls for me, begs for me, and in so doing recalls my responsibility, and calls me into question" (Levinas 1989: 83). The face of the Other is unattainable, but elicits my relationship with the Other as a fellow companion to whom I am committed in a transcendent relation, as the "otherness" of the Other is absolute. A person can be considered a presence of the face; however, they are an incomplete emergence of the face because a person cannot avoid being an unfinished expression of it. Something always escapes a person's figure, and in this way a person is a "caricature," because "being is not only itself, it escapes itself" (Levinas 1989: 135). Consequently, a person is not able to comprehend completely the otherness of the Other; rather, a person becomes an evocation of otherness.

Regarding my connection with Kitty, this meant not to expect knowing everything about her, because in the relationship established with her I just could experience momentary facets of her being in dispersed meetings and conversations. I was able to get glimpses of her and, as we are going to see in a next chapter, she continually found unexpected solutions to her life problems. Yet, through our continuous exchanges, her presence as a face opened up intermittent contact within the fluctuations of her trajectory in São Paulo. Our reciprocal relations expounded my efforts to attend to her call as a face that, by sharing the challenges she endured, showed me how mysterious her being was in the resourcefulness and contradictions of her choices. Kitty was a face that, as I sensed, held a complexity beyond certain conventional portrayals of migrants living in São Paulo.

Kitty as a Face

I met Kitty while I was working at Mr. Kwon's restaurant in Bom Retiro—Mr. Kwon[1] is another important face for this ethnographic work and will be introduced in Chapter 3. The day I first met Kitty was a Friday night, a week before Christmas. All my co-workers, who were originally from Paraguay, had left to celebrate the festive season with their families; only Mr. Kwon, the owner, Mrs. Lee, the manager, and I, the sole employee, were rushing around in the kitchen.

While I was dishwashing, a tall young boy and a petite blonde girl rang the bell and Mrs. Lee immediately opened the restaurant door saying, "They are Wilson's friends."

When they stepped into the kitchen, Mr. Kwon gave them aprons. The girl was directed to the worktop to slice scallions and the boy was given a tray to serve the customers' tables. I joined the girl when she was trimming the bean sprouts and asked her name.

"Kitty," she responded, adding the boy's name: "Jimmy."

The night was busy and I would not meet them again until December 23, 2013. When I arrived at 5:30 p.m. for the night shift, both Kitty and Jimmy had been working in the restaurant since 1 p.m. When I approached Kitty by the sink, she complained that she and Jimmy had been working from 1p.m. to 11p.m. over the weekend. She was exhausted and concerned that the wages were too low. She asked me how much I was given and we confirmed that both of us were offered the

---

1.   I maintained the honorific pronoun for this interlocutor because this was how most locals referred to him: as a senior and respected person.

same amount for two work shifts per day. Prompted by her complaints of low wage, I inquired whether she had had a better salary in a previous job.

Rinsing some bowls, she wiped the sweat from her forehead and commented in Spanish, "Yes, at the *passadera*,[2] we earned more." I continued the conversation by asking what she and Jimmy did in the passadera. She smiled proudly and said, "I ironed the clothes and he folded them." What had happened? Why were they not working there anymore? She squeezed washing-up liquid onto the worn-out sponge and replied, "There's no orders for the *oficinas*[3] around Christmas."

I joined her in dishwashing, rinsing the cutlery she lathered. Kitty revealed, then, that she and Jimmy were together, but they were not married; she was 26 years old and he was 21. She had been living in São Paulo for four years. Jimmy had lived in the city before and had recently returned. When we finished the dishwashing, she showed me a picture of her ten-year-old son on her mobile phone. Her child was in Paraguay with her mother.

Migrants from Paraguay are recurrently characterized as an "invisible" group (Souchaud 2011, Maldonado 2016) in comparison to migrants of other nationalities living in Brazil. Although there are official records of Paraguayans living in the country since the 1940s and a historical migration pattern similar to migrants from Bolivia, the presence of those who were born in

---

2. Outsourced small businesses linked to the clothing industry in Bom Retiro specialized in ironing and folding clothes.

3. *Oficinas* are the outsourced small businesses for the sewing stage in the clothing industry in Bom Retiro. They are usually featured in mass media as "sweatshops."

Paraguay is indistinctly perceived by Brazilian society in general, possibly because of the modest overall number of Paraguayan nationals living in the country. Historically, migrants from Paraguay were concentrated in border towns, such as Foz do Iguaçu or Ponta Porã, but recently significant flows to cities like São Paulo and Rio de Janeiro have been identified since 2000 (Profit 2014). As with many countries in Latin America, Paraguay left a period of military rule in the 1980s and its political and economic restructuring during the 1990s and 2000s did not offer opportunities for prosperity to the new generations (Côrtes 2014). Of those who ventured to go to São Paulo, the majority work in the garment industry, similar to other Latin American nationals from Bolivia and Peru (Côrtes and Silva 2014).

While one can read in Kitty's personal life-journey an expression of the general pattern of Paraguayans in the plural, I aim instead at amplifying the specificity of her trajectory in São Paulo in order to provide a more humane portrayal of her presence, which, as she shared with me, involved not only the search for labor as an economic migrant, but also a search to be desired and loved within the precarious circumstances shaping her trajectory. In not subsuming Kitty's existence to the dominant labels of migrant studies in Brazil, I follow a duty to make her visible in the mundane engagements of her everyday dealings and instabilities, in the indeterminacy of occurrences that shaped her being as a face that insistently puzzled me.

Kitty and I became close workmates during my night shifts in Mr. Kwon's restaurant. We worked well together, completing the tasks Mrs. Lee ordered, organizing ourselves in dishwashing, cutting vegetables, and cleaning the floor. Kitty was the only employee in the restaurant with whom I was able to keep in contact after I left the job. The main means of communication between us became our mobile phones, through a free messaging mobile application, WhatsApp, which is very popular in Brazil. My relationship with Kitty was mostly based on the exchange of WhatsApp messages and intermittent meetings during fieldwork. Her online activity was not intense but she often posted very sensuous pictures of herself on her app profile which mimicked those portraits of vintage femmes fatales. I generally considered this to be an expression of self-esteem and a very authentic part of her personality.

In January 2014, after exchanging messages the day before, Kitty and I were at a corner bar in Bom Retiro. It was Saturday night and the place was abuzz with gales of alcohol-fueled laughter. I offered my glass of *cachaça*,[4] but Kitty ordered a bottle of beer instead. "In Paraguay people are used to *aguardiente*,"[5] she commented. She had just left her work shift at Mr. Kwon's restaurant around 10:30 p.m. After sipping her glass of beer, she asked me, "How was your New Year's Eve?"

"Family, partner, greetings at midnight, nothing special," I said. "How was yours?"

She gulped down the beer and exhaled: "Jimmy locked me in my room when I was to celebrate the night with a female friend. He said he would join his cousins . . . He came, took the keys and left me all alone. I shouted all night long, I tried to phone some friends, but everybody had already gone to party. I threw all Jimmy's stuff out the window. The bastard came back around 5 a.m. . . ."

---

4.   Liquor distilled from sugarcane in Brazil.
5.   Liquor distilled from sugarcane in Paraguay and other Latin American countries.

Shocked by her story, I could not prevent myself from explaining that, if Kitty felt compelled to, she could report Jimmy to the Women's Special Police Office. I would help her to do so. Kitty placed her glass on the table and seeing that I took her too seriously, declared, "No, new year, new life!" She added that Jimmy was not living with her anymore.

In the following weeks, we continued to have brief chats. One day, I noticed that Kitty had changed her phone profile photo and status. The image showed a large female eye with a dripping tear on the corner. The status: "Oh, pain that stabs my heart."

As soon as I noticed it, I texted her: "Hi, are you sad? Do you need help?"

Minutes later, she answered, "The truth, Simone, I tell you, I trust you, I'm pregnant and don't know what to do."

The next morning, as described in the introduction, I met Kitty at the community center where we had that sensitive conversation about what she would like to do, and she could only declare, "I don't know, I don't know . . ." On that day, we bought a pregnancy test together, just to be certain about Kitty's situation. A few days later, she texted me: "Test is positive."

I then wrote back asking, "What do you want to do?"

She took some hours to reply, but late that afternoon she shared a decision: "I want to see Jimmy to decide what to do."

By mid-February, Kitty updated again her profile with a close-up image of the Lady of Caacupé, and no status. When I identified the image of the patron saint of Paraguay, and the blank status on Kitty's app profile, I suspected that her conversation with Jimmy had not gone very well. I immediately texted her again asking how she was. She did not reply, though. For a while, she remained silent and I was left wondering what happened to her. I could not prevent myself from worrying.

This period of silence that lasted about two weeks was a telling expression of the tensions involved in the everyday compromises of Kitty's attachments. It spurred my will to give ethnographic recognition to such an instant, one which was so dramatically experienced by Kitty, but never entirely enunciated by her. Before continuing with Kitty's story, it is necessary to consider the ethnographic grounds required to advance the experimental approach being tailored here—one which incorporates this significant occurrence in her troubled journey in São Paulo.

Ethnography and Evocation

Since the *Writing Culture* debates, anthropologists have been encouraged to reconsider the craft of ethnography by critically examining anthropology's most disseminated writing conventions. The awareness that these standards implied an epistemology that concealed the politics of who represents and who is represented—under the gloss of a supposed scientific objectivity—pushed anthropology to deconstruct the canons that sustained a sense of ethnographic realism. This ethnographic realism was mostly based on the anthropologist's authority of "being there" and their ability to depict culture as a totality in itself. For Clifford (1986), ethnographies are inherently partial truths, because research experience will be at all times fragmented and incomplete. Whereas Clifford suggests forms of substantiating discursive partiality through the usage of fragments and gaps so to emphasize a less holistic mode of knowledge production, Tyler (1986) proposes evocation as a "postmodern" style that is not committed to forms of ethnographic realism either.

Evocation is a significant notion in my ethnographic project since Levinas challenges us to accept the insurmountable alterity of the Other. Recapitulating Levinas's propositions, the Other is unreachable by categories of thought; the Other is an exceeding, a mystery that overflows the thought that is being thought. One respects the radical alterity of the Other, not by the assignment of a category of knowledge that encapsulates the Other, but by invoking the presence of the Other in its "uniqueness." If the Other is not accessed by any category of thought, as Levinas claims, I propose here to refer to the Other through evocation.

For Tyler, "evocation is neither presentation nor representation. It presents no objects and represents none" (1986: 123). In unison with Clifford's critique, Tyler's evocation intends to be an alternative to ethnographic realism and its scientific rhetoric of "objects," "facts," "generalizations," "truth," and similar concepts. As an ethnographic proposal, Tyler's radicalism has been challenging anthropologists to find a way to proceed with evocation as a workable ethnographic operation. More recently, non-representational theories have been responding to some of the questions posed by the *Writing Culture* debate and the crisis of representation.

Concurrent to the awareness that new ethnographic practices are needed because new understandings of what life or the world is require new epistemological grounds, non-representational theorists acknowledge that we live in a world which we can only partially understand. Since, for them, human life is essentially movement, "non-representational theory tries to capture the 'onflow' [. . .] of everyday life" (Thrift 2008: 7). It emphasizes "the fleeting, viscous, lively, embodied, material, more-than-human, precognitive, non-discursive dimensions of spatially and temporally complex lifeworlds" (Vaninni 2015b: 317). Coinciding with Tyler's (1987) concern with the "unspeakable," it also gives importance to what lacks explicit articulation and leaves room for the ephemeral, the fleeting, and the not-quite-graspable. In contrast, non-representational theory does not refute representation as Tyler does; rather, by not pursuing the rendition of the world in realist modes, it requires "representational ethnographers to consider their work to be impressionistic and inevitably creative" (Vaninni 2015b: 318). In not aiming to mimic realities, non-representational ethnographies strive to "animate" lifeworlds by rendering them with new vitality and calling for the engagement of creativity and the imagination as necessary ethnographic practices.

The kind of evocation that I found necessary to do justice to the lives of international mobile actors I met in São Paulo requires imagination as a fundamental element for endeavoring a new ethnographic approach. Evocation in this book will be associated with imagination and push the limits of what Clifford (1986) remarks about ethnographic writings being "fiction," what Tyler suggests as "an emergent fantasy of a possible world of common sense reality" (1986: 126), and what Vaninni proposes as an "irrealist mood" (2015a). In what follows, evocation is a form of enlivening representation that is:

> less concerned with faithfully and detachedly reporting facts, experiences, actions, and situations and more interested instead in making them come to life, in allowing them to take on new and unpredictable meanings, in violating expectations, in rendering them (on paper and other media) through a spirited verve and an élan that reverberates

differently among each different reader, listener, viewer, and spectator (Vaninni 2015a: 119).

Thus, in convergence with this aim, this ethnographic experiment intends to open "new practical-imaginative territories" (Thrift 2008: 21) and "generate possibilities for fabulation" (Vaninni 2015b: 320) by moving not "toward abstraction, [. . .] but back to experience" (Tyler 1986: 135). In the case of the international migrants I had the privilege to encounter, I explore in written form their experiences of doubt, hesitation, and hope to evoke their presences as faces that cannot be entirely grasped, reinstating the liveliness of their unstable trajectories.

"I don't know, I don't know . . ."

As I have already stated at the introduction, the migrants I followed in the metropolitan area of São Paulo in Brazil and beyond repeatedly showed me how their life trajectories were interposed by moments of uncertainty that revealed the intensity and the entanglements of what it is to be alive. In some of these not-yet-articulate instances, people's awareness of their situations allowed their lives to keep going, as was the case with Kitty in her indecision about her pregnancy. There is a richness in this process that is worth appreciating to acknowledge how gaps, pauses, interruptions, and non-defined moments of all sorts are integral to life´s motion. Such moments of inarticulacy may be ephemeral ones. They are not manifestations of anything definitive; they are deeply imbued in ambiguity, vagueness, and contradiction. However, they express the attempt to make sense of the torrents of life itself. Gaining consciousness in such a way, even without a complete enunciation, prompts one to innovatively find new understandings of oneself and the world, reconfiguring the grounds of one's own agency.

In Kitty's case, her silence, performed via a mobile phone app, was the moment when I imagined Kitty becoming aware that the man who was also responsible for her pregnancy was not going to support her. Being alone in São Paulo, the pregnancy would more than likely disrupt Kitty's prior plans of working in Brazil and sending remittances to her ten-year-old son and mother in Paraguay. For unstated reasons, she did not consider Paraguay and her mother's house an option. Moreover, Kitty did not have official documents to stay in Brazil and she worked informally in a restaurant owned by nationals from South Korea. The pregnancy would reinforce the precarious conditions of Kitty's life in São Paulo. Intriguingly, Kitty appealed to the divine grace of a power beyond human jurisdiction, the compassion of Our Lady of Caacupé.[6] Renewing this connection through the mediation of a mobile phone app, she made partially public, for those who were part of her social media network, something about her state at that moment.

Other trajectories that I followed during fieldwork, narrated in the following chapters, showed how migrants lives become open-ended experiences, with diversions and unexpected occurrences. Life finds itself to be an immense and inescapable torrent, interspersed with points of doubt, hesitation, silence, or anxiety. In most cases, these moments were barely voiced by my

6. Also known as Our Lady of Miracles, the Lady of Caacupé is one of the most celebrated patron saints in Paraguay, whose sanctuary is located in the city of Caacupé.

interlocutors. Still, they were suggestive of this openness in which the subjective and the social, the conscious and the unconscious, seemed to merge and overlap, allowing existence to be reconstituted or innovated.

For Hastrup, it is through the "inarticulate mind" that anthropology has the opportunity to "reclaim the areas of silence as a basis for understanding agency" (1995: 193). As a dynamic zone of contact, the mind is partially articulate, having a proportion of knowledge that remains inaccessible to others. In venturing towards the inarticulate, I acknowledge that life in its very process of becoming is composed of nebulous moments of awareness and, simultaneously, its deficient understandings are part of people's relations in and with the world.

The process of understanding what it is not entirely expressed is possible if the inarticulate is deemed part of human experience: a form of the immediate realization of the world in the subtle way it is individually and momentarily lived, and through which consciousness permeates experience in the process of living. Consciousness in anthropology came to be a sensitive notion, questioning, as it does, the dichotomies between the individual and the social, the body and the mind, the inner and the outer person (Cohen and Rapport 1995). But it also offers the opportunity to attentively consider the interplay between the subjective, the social, and the mind. In the present analysis, the experimental approach developed here aims at enabling an incorporation of the inarticulate moments in certain life trajectories, inspiring a way of understanding beyond a positivist scientific standard.

In this line, I explore Bergson's and Dilthey's considerations of different aspects of consciousness and knowledge. They offered insight on the theme of immediate knowledge as a foundational ground. This concerned the place of freedom in human consciousness, for the former, and the specificity of human sciences in relation to the natural sciences, for the latter. Contrary to a Kantian assumption that the human mind is constituted by a priori categories organizing the way that people apprehend reality and organize the world, Bergson (1959a) posited the presence of a realm in consciousness that is prior to any classification. In the depths of consciousness, different "états *de conscience*" (states of consciousness) can be operative. There is the domain in which the immediate experience is lived in the multiplicity of "*faits de conscience*" (facts of consciousness). This multiplicity exists simultaneously in a very peculiar temporality called "*durée*." In the pure durée, it is not possible to attribute name, relation, or definition to any fact of consciousness. These are operations afforded in a subsequent stage by consciousness. For this reason, this state of consciousness is prior to the presence of language or abstract reasoning, for example. Although it is a highly inarticulate state of consciousness, it is in the durée that the experience of freedom is available. For Bergson (1959b), there lies in the multiplicity of the durée the possibility to generate a creative stance toward life, which he refers to as the "élan vital" (vital tone).

Whereas Bergson's concern with the immediate data of consciousness stimulates an attention to the reticent moments lived by my interlocutors, Dilthey considers these experiences as part of the complex activity of producing understanding throughout the process of life. In considering all lived experiences of things, thoughts, or feelings as "facts of consciousness," Dilthey proposed the existence of immediate awareness: a "pre-reflexive mode of self-givenness in which the dichotomies of form and content, subject and object characteristic of reflexive consciousness do not exist" (1989 [1883]: 247). For him, as for Bergson, consciousness is not restricted only to representational and intellectual operations. However, "facts have their existence only within consciousness" (Dilthey 1989 [1883]: 277). In defining experience as the fundamental aspect of human understanding, Dilthey (2002 [1910]) attaches the very processes of knowing to the movement of life itself. The course of a life consists of lived experiences connected to each other through consciousness, i.e., experiences that are facts of consciousness. This "nexus" of facts of consciousness is linked to the continuum that makes one's life, which is composed of the nexus of past-present-future implications, the nexus of relations with other beings, and the nexus of external organizations, such as associations or governments (and other nexuses). For Dilthey, the pursuit of a science that is committed to taking into account human processes of consciousness requires the explication of the structural articulation of these points of connectedness.

In unfolding this ethnographic experiment, I am interested in making visible how the unclear moments of experience are aspects of consciousness that can be revelatory of how someone can reach new awareness of her life, and so keep going. In this undertaking, I draw on Bergson's ideas of the durée and élan vital to begin to understand how these imprecise moments of consciousness can impart new vivacity to someone's life, recognizing life as an ongoing venture. In turn, Dilthey's elaboration of the pre-objective experience—a range that spans from the "most rudimentary level prior to analytical separation of the subject and object (erleben)" (Ermarth 1978: 130) to the most clarified and objective ones—further supports my considerations on the connectedness of this realm to other structures of life. In particular, Dilthey's hermeneutic procedure encourages my ethnography to disclose the connectedness between moments of consciousness—even the most opaque ones—and the making of someone's life.

Evoking the Other through Experience and Imagination

Whereas I intend to make visible the fleeting moments of consciousness observed in some of my interlocutors' trajectories, this will be ethnographically implemented through the engagement of my own subjectivity as well, following Levinas's advice to attend to the Other's call by conjuring it as a face.

As we saw above, Dilthey (2002 [1910]) proposes hermeneutics as a process of understanding and interpreting the connections between consciousness and experience. Understanding and interpretation are based on the singularity of individual existences that, through the intelligibility of their own inner lived experiences, are able to develop a self-understanding that emerges when appreciating other lives. In other words, understanding others is possible only through the transposition of one's own lived experiences in the re-creation of the connectedness of someone else's lived experiences. This re-experiencing of others' plausible states of mind is necessary because the existence of others is "given only from the outside, in sensory events, gestures, words, and actions" (Dilthey and Jameson 1972: 231). Thus, in such re-comprehension of other people's experiences, everything must be translated out of one's own sense of life.

In this ethnographic experiment, Dilthey's hermeneutics of connectedness through consciousness and experience establishes the fundamental aspect of a mode of evocation: the understanding that everyone shares a common condition of consciousness that enables them to enliven within themselves experiences that others have been through. From this elementary disposition, connectedness will be hereby approached by re-creating it as an experience evoked in the researcher's own inner experience. In other words, in order to understand the lives I followed during fieldwork, I will incorporate the inarticulate moments I attended to in the research process by reanimating these occurrences with resources from my own experiences with the research participants. In this re-experiencing of others' lived experience, imagination is central: it becomes fundamental to this process of understanding. As Dilthey himself stated, "human beings can experience many other kinds of existence through imagination" (2002 [1910]: 237). It is in the use of imagination as a way of understanding in anthropology (Harris and Rapport 2015) that this analysis intends to express the richness of the lives I encountered during fieldwork.

However, Dilthey's hermeneutics justifies the adoption of imagination as a way of ethnographically recreating the lived experience of others—a way to regain the connectedness of the lives of research subjects—*rather than* as a means of discerning the meaning of research subjects' intentions. In the experiment of this ethnography, by contrast, I engage a hermeneutics of connectedness instead of a hermeneutics of signification. This emphasis on regaining the connectedness inherent in the making of people's lives meets Levinas's assertion that a relationship with the Other is essentially ethical before the irreducibility of the Other. Inasmuch as it is not possible to determine the meanings arising from the Other, there remains the task of interpreting how an inchoate incident is connected to the making of someone's life. However, this connectedness, as inspired by Dilthey's hermeneutics, entails eliciting a relationship with the Other by a process of sensing the Other through one's own inner experiences. Thus, connectedness is not substantiation—elucidating the substance of another's meaningful life—it is evocation.

In broadening the scope of what is knowable in human affairs by including the most tenuous forms of consciousness, Bergson and Dilthey open up a horizon of possibilities for understanding life experience as a continuous movement of making sense of self, the Other, and the world. As Throop urges, the examination of experiences that "reside on the fringes of our abilities to articulate, verbalize and interpret" may "allow researchers to investigate in finer detail those modes of experience that lie on the peripheries of the patterning imperatives of our attentional modalities" (2002: 19).

At this point, not only does the act of understanding become central to maintaining the course of a human life in itself, but it equally makes plausible an approach that uses imagination as a way to comprehend the experiences of other human beings. Although Levinas (1967, 1987) reminds us that knowing may well be an unattainable operation in the face of the Other, the effort cannot be in vain. In the end, it might be at least a form of recognition, of attendance and appreciation.

Aesthetics as an Experimental Way of Evocation

As formulated above, imagination in this ethnographic account evokes the experiences of others. More precisely, imagination appears in this ethnographic experiment though aesthetics. Here, writing is the chosen media to make aesthetically perceptible certain inarticulate instances in the lives of my interlocutors. Again, Dilthey's work encourages me to outline a proposal with support from Dewey's ideas about experience and aesthetics. Dilthey (1985 [1887]) believes that the source of all artistic creation is lived experience. Imagination cannot arise from a vacuum: it works from the facts of life and applies cognitive transformations to them. The aesthetic procedure secures the intensity of lived experience to be appreciated through objects of art. Artworks, in fact, disclose a "sense of life" and "vitality" through "reverberating" the emotion of an individual human life (Dilthey 1985 [1887]: 60). Similarly, but more radically, Dewey considered the experience of living as aesthetic experience *per se*. An experience is the outcome of "the interaction of live creature and environing conditions", which, by being integrated into the "stream of experiences from other experiences" reaches a completeness in its consummation that turns it into "*an* experience" (1980 [1934]: 35–37). The aesthetic experience is the one in which fulfillment is achieved in such a manner that the whole creature feels alive. Experience then is already "heightened vitality," and as "the fulfillment of an organism in its struggle and achievement in a world of things, it is art in germ. Even in its rudimentary forms, it contains the promise of that delightful perception which is aesthetic experience" (1980 [1934]: 18–19).

Imagination, in this view, is constitutive of all conscious experience for the reason that the course of life in its movement is also made of gaps within the many experiences. Imagination plays the decisive role in supporting the living creature in speculating on possible understandings in order to connect across gaps and thus to venture into what is unknown. In the aesthetic experience of life, the restatement of meanings through imagination is crucial because it grants consciousness the perception of the flow of life and, at the same time, the awareness of the interruptions in its flux that fuels the feeling of being fresh and alive (Dewey 1980 [1934]: 54).

Inspired by the "sense of life," "vitality," and "being alive" suggested by Dilthey and Dewey, this ethnographic experiment is animated by the adoption of an aesthetic approach to make sense of the richness found in migrants' lives. As Dewey writes: "Tangled scenes of life are made more intelligible in aesthetic experience: not, however, as reflection and science render things more intelligible by reduction to conceptual form, but by presenting their meanings as the matter of clarified, coherent, and intensified or 'impassionate' experience" (1980 [1934]: 302).

Previously, I mentioned Dilthey´s hermeneutics as a window to understanding the *connectedness* of people's experiences through the use of imagination. Reiterating this point, it relates to the notion of imagination as a means of recreating the sense of *vitality* in human life. Thus, imagination here is not exactly a "path" that reaches knowledge by making life more intelligible. Imagination is rather an openness that makes life something re-inhabited as vibrant and vivacious through the mediation of lived experience. In this way, it becomes more an invitation to appreciate, rather than disclose, the human, following Levinas's acknowledgment of the irreducibility of the Other and our responsibility to attend this presence without turning it into an object.

In brief, the aesthetic approach developed here intends to broaden the understanding of my interlocutors' experiences in the making of their lives by reconstituting the integrity, i.e., the vitality, of their involvements by recourse to imagination—mine and theirs. Imagination will be substantiated in snippets of fictional narratives that are intended to show the connectedness of specific experiences to other levels of human relatedness, as will be developed in the coming section and chapters.

The Poetics of Resonance: An Experiment in Anthropology through Imagination

The aesthetic operation in which I deploy imagination as a way of appreciating the human in this ethnographic experiment will be designated here as a "poetics of resonance." The poetics of resonance recognizes the instability associated with existence and the vitality embedded in the intricacies of life processes. It therefore indicates the plausibility of understanding as a provisional proposal of recognition and approximation at best. As an approximation directed to apprehend those pieces of inarticulate human expression that constitute the richness of someone's life, the poetics of resonance aims to capture this generous dimension of imagination. It gives an account of how life in its precarious and impermanent moments can be embraced with all the incongruity, inconsistency, and confusion involved. In animating these fading instances, this poetics aims to integrate what seems to be incongruous in life itself, reconstituting its complexity in ambiguity and contradiction. *To know through the poetics of imagination is to know through "resonance" in the sense that while one might not be able objectively to reason about people's lives and experiences, one can subjectively intuit or sense what it is like to live a particular life or experience in its richness.*

"Poetics" here refers to the aesthetic operation of converting lived experience into written expression. Since I as an author do this by relying on both my and others' experiences, the poetics here undertaken alludes to Bakhtin's (1981) idea of "heteroglossia," which is the acknowledgment of the convergence of diverse discursive presences in the same linguistic expression. The most relevant aspect of Bakhtinian heteroglossia for this poetics is the "double-voiced discourse": As Bakhtin writes:

> Heteroglossia [. . .] is another's speech in another's language, serving to express authorial intentions but in a refracted way. Such speech constitutes a special type of double-voiced discourse. It serves two speakers at the same time and expresses simultaneously two different intentions: the direct intention of the character who is speaking, and the refracted intention of the author. In such discourse there are two voices, two meanings and two expressions. And all the while these two voices are dialogically interrelated, they—as it were—know about each other (just as two exchanges in a dialogue know of each other and are structured in this mutual knowledge of each other); it is as if they actually hold a conversation with each other. Double-voiced discourse is always internally dialogized. [. . .] A potential dialogue is embedded in them, one as yet unfolded, a concentrated dialogue of two voices, two world views, two languages (1981: 324).

To transfigure another's experience through such poetics requires an alternative dialogue between my authorial consciousness and the others' (authorial) consciousnesses, a dialogue that is believed to be possible by way of the notion of resonance *as an aesthetic and ethical mediation*. "Resonance" in this poetics means the capacity that one has to be affected by the expressions of feelings and experiences of others given that these feelings and experiences can be evoked in oneself. The aesthetic effect is to elicit in oneself the experience another has gone through in such a way that, in conveying that experience through this poetics, others—the readers—may go through a similar experience.

Wikan (2012) gained insight into feelings of resonance through conversations with Balinese scholars. They advised her to create "resonance" in herself with the people and their problems in order to convey to the world what the Balinese were like. From a Balinese standpoint, resonance was a sort of understanding embedded deeply in sentiments of empathy or compassion; it was "a willingness to *engage* with another world, life, or idea; an ability to use one's experience [. . .] to try to grasp, or convey, meanings that do not reside in words, 'facts', nor text but are evoked in the meeting of one experiencing subject with another or with a text" (Wikan 2012: 57).

In my ethnographic experiment, resonance is the approach by which I found a means to bring to light the fleeting moments of perplexity or ambiguity that were recurrently experienced in the lives I followed during fieldwork. This empathic process of understanding shares with Wikan's notion the intention of grasping meanings that are conveyed "beyond words." However, resonance in this ethnography is also an ethical mediation in the sense asserted by Levinas (1967), the kind of possible relationship between me and the irreducibility of the Other. In recognizing the impossibility of reaching the Other through knowledge, I invoke the sensations and experiences that allow me to imagine how it might feel to be in a particular person's place, conscious that I will never entirely know how it is for sure. Thus, resonance is this willingness to recognize and appreciate the presence of another person, despite the unattainability of knowing this person completely.

Interferences within resonance are multiple. Throop (2010) examined how his experiences of grief affected his relations with and perceptions of the Yap people he had been researching for a long time. He referred to the seminal contribution from Renato Rosaldo (1989), which argues that one gains insight into people's understandings through the empathetic process of going through similar experiences. Throop identified that, in holding homologous sentiments of bereavement when attending funerals on the Island of Yap, his emotional state surely opened new focuses of awareness about the changes in the Yapese groups he was observing. However, "empathetic resonance," as he called it, with the bereaved was not something that transparently opened a completely new comprehension of the Yapese. Quite the reverse: empathy was a course punctuated by moments of distancing, confusion, and displacement as well. As a result, "empathetic resonance" is a process gained through time (see also Hollan 2008), impregnated with obscure moments that intermittently allow new empathetic moments to take place. Acknowledging the limitations of empathetic processes before the irreducibility of beings, situations, or moments, my notion of resonance is an approximation, not a transparent connection.

For the purposes of this ethnographic experiment, *resonance is this capacity people have to be affected by others and the world.* It takes the form of invoking a sense of appreciation between oneself, others, and the world. Simultaneously, one's own act of resonance can, in turn, affect others and the world by further "reverberation." Resonance and reverberation are co-related operations in the sense that at the same time that one is affected by others and the world, one may manifest these effects through oneself. However, resonance and reverberation are not necessarily the same. *Reverberation is the voluntary or involuntary manifestation of the way someone has been affected by others and the world, possibly affecting others and the world as well.*

Resorting to Dilthey's hermeneutics as explained previously, resonance is the process of apprehending other lives by connecting other people's experiences to one's own inner experiences. In re-experiencing others' existences through one's own lived experiences, a particular and personal understanding of people's lives is made possible. This understanding can be expressed back to others and the world as reverberation, offering another possibility for others and the world to engage with it or not. Thus, experience is the fundamental element that constitutes people's capacities to resonate and reverberate. Resonance and reverberation in this way are not physical operations or forms of communication, but, drawing on Levinas, they are forms of evocation based on people's personal experiences. Through this evocation, people may (or may not) be able to recognize the Other or the world as a worthwhile presence with whom to establish (or not) an ethical and reciprocal attitude.

For the moment, it suffices to emphasize that the notions of resonance and reverberation provide a trope to consider life as a vibrating venture, in which each being has a particular frequency of movement because of specific sets of experiences. In reverberating a determined frequency of experience, one being can influence the vibration of others. The ones struck by it may change their vibration or not depending on the quality of the experiences they have already had. As long as the tuning in to another's frequency occurs, one is able to enliven in oneself a version of the other's experience. By using the metaphor of soundwaves, my intention is to clarify how the idea of resonance operates at a conceptual level, as the kind of empathic attitude I am conveying here is not a physical phenomenon.

Having outlined what "poetics" and "resonance" mean in my approach, it is necessary, however, to indicate how the poetics of resonance materialize in my text. Although the imaginative process evoke specific impressions, it does not aspire to "fill in the gaps" by allocating words, feelings, or deeds to research subjects in the manner of a ventriloquist's work. The poetics of resonance intends to instigate in the reader a perception of inchoate manifestations of human experience. It hopes to do so by amplifying their existence—and, in so doing, portray the lives of those whom I met with a sense of vitality and complexity. As mentioned before, the poetics of resonance intends to affect the reader by transforming what resonated in me from different research participants into imaginative pieces of writing. These pieces of fiction, then, become deliberate attempts at reverberation that may or may not instigate something in the reader. At least, there remains the invitation to connect.

The poetics of resonance thus takes concrete form in this ethnographic experiment through fragments of fictional narratives that are based on the data and observations I gathered during fieldwork. In other words, here are micro-stories as expressions of how each singular encounter resonated in me. These short fictions convey those very instances when people are generating the necessary nexuses involved in the making of their lives and gaining awareness of their situations. In these moments, a person may become sensible of her own reaches and legacies oscillating in scenarios of limitation and potentiality. At these sensitive points, my hope is that it is possible to glimpse the richness and the roughness of leading a life. In appreciating the density of people's existences, anthropology can be aware of the capacities involved in making a life, and all the entanglements this entails. It is in the density of a life that the potentialities and inventiveness for overcoming predicaments or generating new forms of existence in the world resides.

The fictionalized stories will appear throughout the book in grey boxes as amplifying instruments. Respecting their inner rationale as fiction, and the epistemological distance imputed in them as means for appreciating people's lives, the imaginative narratives will be based on the people and situations I encountered during my fieldwork, but some parts of these narratives will be written for the effect of fictionalizing each experience and making visible those unspoken moments of uncertainty and concern. In this line, the fictionalized sections are not "true" in the sense of reproducing witnessed acts or facts, but they *are* true as ways to recreate the vitality intrinsic to life as I experienced it alongside some of my research interlocutors in the field.

Finally, we reach the point where we can go back to Kitty's silence and engage with such a uncertain moment in her life through the poetics of resonance.

Selfie[7]

Ay, nena, como estás guapa con tu pelo cayéndote sobre los hombros. Ay, boquita roja, da ganas de morder. Mira esos ojos de avellana . . . un peligro, tigresa. Sí, Kitty, ahora como Marilyn Monroe, brazos cerca de tu cuello

---

7. A version of this fictional piece first appeared in Toji (2023).

*y la boca haciendo pucheritos. Linda. Sonrisa seductora,
casi Angelina Jolie.*[8]

Kitty posed alone in front of the full-length mirror
and captured frames of herself with the mobile. She was
searching for the best angle by moving her right arm
down and left shoulder up. *Ah, ya está.*[9] She chose the
photo in which she's sitting on the bed, covered only by
the beige sheet of purple flowers, legs half-open, long
hair loose over her right shoulder. It did not look like she
had just woken up. She posted the image and wrote:
"Sólo el verdadero amor salva."[10]

Then, she waited.

*

No sign of Jimmy. He did not come to sleep that night,
did not respond to her messages, nor did he like her
photos. She called his mobile several times and nothing. She just saw him again at work at Mr Kwon's
restaurant.

Jimmy came in smiling, with his peroxide blonde hair
and worn-out jeans, bouncing confidence: "Hola."[11] He
did not even have time to justify himself to Kitty; maybe
he had not even have thought about it.

---

8. Spanish: Oh, baby, how beautiful you are with your hair
     falling on your shoulders. Yeah, this little red mouth,
     it makes one crazy to bite. Now, look at those almond
     eyes . . . a danger, tigress. Yes, Kitty, now like Marilyn
     Monroe, arms close to your neck and mouth pouting.
     Cute. Seductive smile, almost Angelina Jolie.
9. Spanish: Oh, that's it.
10. Spanish: Only true love saves.
11. Spanish: Hello.

He received the apron and tray from Mr Kwon's hands, who immediately dispatched him to the customers without hesitation: "Table 10." Kitty remained in the kitchen chopping chives and followed Jimmy's silver hair travelling among the tables of the restaurant.

Meanwhile, Ms Lee lost patience with her team of Paraguayan assistants: "Ay, no, donde está lechuga? Kitty, tijeras. Anda, procura tijeras. Francisco, kimchi, kimchi, traz."[12]

Kitty hurriedly wiped her hands on the apron and searched the kitchen for the scissors. She cursed in low voice: "Coreana miserable, quince años en Paraguay, y todavia no habla un rato de español decente. Y ahora viviendo aqui en San Pablo no habla portugués tampoco."[13]

Finally, Kitty found the scissors under the dishwasher and, still wet, she handed them to Mr Lee, who immediately cut the *pajeón*[14] into symmetrical squares to go to the customers. The bell of the restaurant rang, signalling the presence of other customers at the barred entrance. Kitty glanced towards the security circuit TV while cleaning the bean sprouts. On the black-and-white screen, she squeezed her eyes and could not make out anything very well.

---

12. Spanish: Oh, no, where's the lettuce? Kitty, scissors. Go, get scissors. Francisco, kimchi, kimchi, bring it.

13. Spanish: Miserable Korean, fifteen years in Paraguay and she still doesn't speak decent Spanish. And now living here in São Paulo she doesn't speak Portuguese either.

14. Korean dish made from a batter of eggs, wheat and rice flour, scallions and often other ingredients depending on the variety.

Because of the delay in opening the door, Ms Lee shouted at her, "Brasisero o coreano?"[15] Kitty continued looking at the screen, and without getting any response, Ms. Lee got impatient and went herself to see the TV: "Ay, son brasireros . . . Passa, Caty, avísales que el restaurante está cerrando, que no hay más comida."[16]

Kitty went to lie to the unwanted visitors with her precarious *Portunhol*[17]: "Perdón, se há fetchado todo."[18] Returning to the kitchen, she saw Jimmy across the hall. He did not even smile at her and continued to serve the tables as if she were not there, because there, in fact, only the Korean customers' desires mattered.

At the end of the day, Jimmy, of course, was not waiting for her.

*

Hermosa, eres irresistible! Sueltas tu pelo sedoso y vuelves tu rostro hacia el lado. Sí, linda. Cierra los ojos y sopla un besito con tu mano derecha. No te olvides de flexionar tu cintura para la izquierda. Um ratito más para la izquierda, más y . . . Dale.[19]

---

15. Accented Spanish: Brazilian or Korean?
16. Spanish: Oh, they're Brazilians . . . Go, Kitty, tell them that the restaurant is closing, that there's no more food.
17. The Portunhol is a hybrid of Spanish and Portuguese.
18. Portunhol: Sorry, everything is now closed.
19. Spanish: Beauty, you are irresistible! Loosen your silky hair and turn your face to the left. Yes, great, close your eyes and blow a kiss with your right hand. Do not forget to bend your waist to the left. A little more to the left, more and . . . Yes!

Kitty pressed the button on her mobile and was pleased with that image of herself. She updated her post and wrote: "Cuando el amor es eterno, nada más importa."[20]

Then she pressed a kiss on the mobile screen. Whoever noticed the left corner of the picture would see the almost imperceptible part of a window. From that corner, the broken glass let in a heart-shivering cold wind. But Kitty did not perceive it.

*

God, she could not believe it when she realized that the door latch turned. Her heart accelerated, and when she saw that Jimmy was entering the room, she could not prevent herself from shouting with joy. It was New Year's Eve and she hadn't seen him for ages. She had just put on her white polka-dot dress and was about to apply some lipstick in front of the mirror. She was getting ready to leave with other Paraguayans who wanted to take advantage of the New Year's celebration on Paulista Avenue.

Nívea came to call her from the corridor, but without even opening the door, Kitty hugged Jimmy and simply shouted out, "No, nena, me quedo acá, gracias!"[21] Jimmy smiled at her and placed the kiss on her mouth that she was desperately longing for. *Ay, diós mio.*[22]

Both fell on the creased bed. Jimmy unzipped his shabby jeans and then nested himself between Kitty's legs. Kitty did not have time to understand what had

---

20. Spanish: When love is eternal, nothing else matters.
21. Spanish: No, dear, I'm staying here, thank you!
22. Spanish: Oh, my god.

happened, but she was glad to have Jimmy back in her room that night.

She just did not expect him to get up, close the zipper and tell her, "Me voy a celebrar con mis hermanos."[23] He went to the bedroom door, took Kitty's keys from the latch and locked the door from outside.

Kitty, still dishevelled, could not believe what was happening. "Jimmy, Jimmy", she screamed while forcing the lock on the door without success. "Jimmy, no me dejes sola, por diós!"[24]

She decided to call for Nívea, but her friend had already left. She yelled for help in case there was somebody left in one of the other little rooms. But nothing, no one. She did not dare to scream out the window; she didn't have the papers to stay and so was afraid that the police would come. She became infuriated and began to put together everything that belonged to Jimmy, the black Mizoono[25] cap, the Men Active deodorant, the blue Calvin Clein[26] underwear. She took what was his and hurled it through the window facing a car park.

When Kitty realized that the fireworks were bursting across the city, she could not bear the commotion in her ears and started to scream out loud. She began the new year already breathless and voiceless.

*

---

23. Spanish: I'm going to celebrate with my brothers.
24. Spanish: Jimmy, don't leave me alone, I beg you!
25. Reference to cheap products imitating those of famous brands.
26. Another reference to cheap products imitating those of famous brands.

Nena, no veo nada diferente. Estás linda como siempre. Piel satinada, pelos brillantes, lábios suaves.[27] Kitty circled her mobile phone around herself, examining the moving image carefully. *Continúas muy guapa.*[28] She held the device for a moment at waist height, and pulled in her belly. She shrank it a little further and lifted the mobile to her head again. She drew the phone closer to her right eye, but the camera could not focus so close; she clicked the blurred image of her honey-coloured pupil. She posted the photo and typed: "El amor es ciego."[29]

*

In the restaurant, usually, there was not a second's respite. Kitty and her colleagues cut the vegetables, washed the utensils, carried out the trash. When the house was at its full capacity, no way.

But that day, as soon as she stepped into the kitchen, Kitty was summoned by Ms Lee: "Kitty, Jimmy dice que estás embarazada, así no quiere, señor Kwon le paga el mes."[30] Kitty tried to argue that she could still work and needed that job, but Ms. Lee was emphatic: "Así no quiere, no quiere."[31]

Kitty wanted to be in Jimmy's arms and, now that she carried a child in her womb, she hoped to bring him definitely into her life. Sitting on her bed, she called his

---

27. Spanish: Baby, I do not see anything different. You look pretty as always. Satin skin, shiny hair, soft lips.
28. Spanish: You are still very beautiful.
29. Spanish: Love is blind.
30. Spanish: Kitty, Jimmy says you're pregnant. We don't want you like this. Mr. Kim will pay you the month.
31. Spanish: Like this, we don't want you, we don't want you.

number on her mobile phone and waited. It rang once, twice, it rang three times. It rang for the fourth time and Kitty was fading inside. It rang for the fifth time and, to her surprise, the bastard answered. Kitty had a moment of rapture.

However, it lasted only a second, because the voice on the other side did not even give her room to murmur a hello. It was like a slap on her face: "Carajo, no me molestes, estoy con mi novia!"[32]

And he hung up on her.

Kitty kept the phone in her hands. She breathed once, twice, and did not feel she was alive. She turned on the camera mode and looked at the device's screen. She looked and stared at the image of her own face, observed how the screen amplified her protruding belly and thick legs. She felt ugly, fat and alone. She chose not to take any photo and continued to follow the mobile screen, now exploring her feet, the bed and the floor of her bedroom. She noticed the worn-out mattress and the damp beaten floor. She pointed to the red closet without a door, the grimy two-burner stove and the tiny space between the bed and the door. Without work, the pots remained empty on the tiny improvised sink. From the window, light burst through the screen in white torrents. At the corner of the window, she recovered the image of her *Virgen de Caacupé*. It was the size of a beer can. She turned her mobile phone to the saint, framed it in full screen and pressed the button. She posted the photo but did not write anything that day. She just joined her hands on the right side, pressed the phone to her chest, and fell for a silent and inspired prayer.

---

32. Spanish: Fuck, don't bother me, I'm with my girlfriend!

Kitty may not have gone through such inward distress; this may be too dramatic to be true. But by vivifying this moment of silence, the poetics of resonance emphasizes the existence of such instant. Nonetheless, as a fictional act, it keeps the mystery of Kitty's situation, as much as it triggers our imagination suggestively. From here onwards, a poetics of resonance, as I have named it, will be spread throughout the coming chapters, hopefully replenishing aesthetically what is often overlooked by scholarly accounts but makes an interlocutor's trajectory a unique transformative process, as we are going to discuss.

CHAPTER 2

Being Singular

De perto, ninguém é normal.[1]
Caetano Veloso, *Vaca Profana*, 1986.

The imponderabilia of actual life invites, as I have discussed, the crafting of an ethnographic disposition that is mindful of the limitations of any act of knowledge before the instability embedded in one's interlocutors' circumstances and their existences as faces. As a means of ethical approximation, and not scientific disclosure, a poetics of resonance privileges an empathetic attendance towards my interlocutors' particular situations. In this chapter, I delineate more accurately how this poetics requires ethnographic care to each research participant's singularity. Where Kitty was our companion in the preceding part, Mr. Kwon and Helen now become

---

1. Up close, no one is normal.

our guides in the minutiae of their personal trajectories in São Paulo.

Uniqueness, Singularity, and Methodological Irreducibility

Both Mr. Kwon and Helen were born in South Korea; although this research avoids nationality as an explanatory category, most studies about migrants in São Paulo would probably consider them under the category of Koreans. The literature about Koreans in Latin America and Brazil documents that the first groups of Koreans moved to countries such as Argentina, Brazil and Paraguay during the 1960s due to official emigration policies supported by the South Korean government following the Korean War (Choi 1991, Park 2014). After the failed efforts of state-led initiatives, Koreans in search of new life possibilities continued to travel at their own expense, independently creating informal migratory networks in the countries of their destination. In Brazil, the majority of migrants coming from South Korea concentrated in the city of São Paulo, becoming increasingly involved in the clothing industries of central neighborhoods such as Bom Retiro and Brás (Choi 2009, Chi 2016b). However, many of these migrant families had also been open to moving to places with better economic opportunities in addition to countries such as Paraguay, Argentina or Brazil and some of their members later migrated to countries such as the United States or Canada, making a "transnational space" for the circulation of Koreans between countries of South and North America (Park 1999 and 2014, Monteiro and Bastos 2011).

The lives of Mr. Kwon and Helen, as we are going to see below, are in dialogue with the history and movements described above, but underlining the particularity of their personal trajectories shows how complex and diverse these processes can be when we interrogate, at a microscopic level, the neat and coherent generality of the scholarly terminology. By drawing attention to the singularity of a personal experience, I ethnographically renounce reducing my interlocutors' experiences to a pattern or a general category. As considered in the previous chapter, when I identify the irreducibility of the Other in my relationship with the absolute Other, I am able to recognize the unattainable otherness evoked by someone's presence through her uniqueness (Levinas 1998). In the uniqueness of the expression of a face, I acknowledge the irreducibility of the Other and I am able to glimpse what it means in terms of "infinity," as Levinas calls the metaphysical possibility of existing in absolute otherness. For Levinas, "uniqueness" is "precisely a doing justice to the difference of the other person" (1998: 166), because only the unique is absolutely other. In respecting the singular, we do not appropriate the face of the Other. Convergently, Rapport understands that "the human comprises a complex singularity" (2009: 110), which cannot be overshadowed by categories of ascription or affiliation such as race, class, gender, or religion. In seeing uniqueness as a fundamental ethnographic value, this research about international mobile actors living in the city of São Paulo is not based on classificatory categories such as nationality or ethnic belonging, as is common in migration studies.

Besides considering all interlocutors as international mobile actors living in the city of São Paulo, this ethnographic account rejects general categories of classification in an effort not to reduce research participants to "an object of knowledge" (Rapport and Stade 2007: 229). This ethnographic experiment makes a stand in taking seriously migrants' portrayals of themselves, comprehending the particularity of their existence in their own terms. Therefore, this is not a study about "South Koreans," "migrant women," or "Paraguayan workers." This is an account of some men and women, working-class and middle-class individuals, whom I met directly or indirectly in the neighborhood of Bom Retiro. Some were born in Paraguay or Bolivia, others in South Korea or China, but all of them, as we are going to see, developed very unique life trajectories, which required the crafting of a different ethnographic attitude to do justice to their singularity.

As follows, in this part, I depict how Helen and Mr. Kwon, as faces, call ethical and ethnographic attention to the specifics of their life courses and tribulations, detailing, as I have been doing with Kitty, their heterogenous and disparate trajectories, even while Mr. Kwon and Helen share the same nationality and most probably would have their particularities effaced and anonymized in studies considering them as Koreans in the plural. I see this operation of preserving the personal minutiae of my research interlocutors as a way to accomplish an anthropological account concerned with methodological irreducibility.

"I think, I think . . . ah, I think . . ."

I begin with Helen, who I met on the first day of the Portuguese classes I volunteered to teach in a public school in Bom Retiro on Sundays. She had recently arrived in São Paulo, accompanying her husband, who was a postdoctoral researcher at the University of São Paulo.

She was determined to learn Portuguese and particularly interested in taking the Celpe-Bras test,[2] the official exam for assessing a foreigner's proficiency of Portuguese in Brazil. With a degree in Japanese, she was cognizant of the resources to acquire a new language and a very adept learner. Her husband was born in Brazil, and, although not having a Japanese ancestry, they generally used Japanese at home. Helen met her husband in Japan, when she was teaching Korean to Japanese officials. Her husband, by that time, was studying in a Japanese university for a doctoral degree in Chemistry. In Brazil, they lived in a neighborhood in the west zone of São Paulo, close to the University of São Paulo. As a young couple in their mid-thirties, they had a one-year-old girl, conceived in Japan, but born in South Korea.

I chose to start with Helen's story because her trajectory did not express the usual portrayal of Koreans in the specialized literature, as her move to Brazil was not related to joining Korean kin or exploring business opportunities (Choi 2009; Kim and Lee 2016); she did not live in a neighborhood such as Bom Retiro, Aclimação or Morumbi (Chi 2016a); and she did not look for chances to meet other Koreans in churches, cultural associations, or private schools either, as was frequently the case (Sampaio 2011, Chi 2016a).

I especially valued her self-perception of being *different*, as she once declared over a cup of tea at her house, during a break in one of our private Portuguese classes.

"Actually, I'm not a proper Korean," she said, illustrating this by recalling two episodes in her life. The

2.   This test was established by the Ministry of Education in 2010 and is the language certificate required to study in a Brazilian university or to apply for the naturalization process in the country.

first one sent us back to her childhood, to the small town where her parents still lived, in a time when she amused herself with catching fish or toads with her younger brother in a nearby watercourse; elder ladies would remark to her mother that her daughter was behaving too "boyishly." This memory immediately led her to another one, when she was already a young adult and she joined her parents at her father's elder brother's party. She wanted to meet these relatives again as she had not seen them for years after leaving to Japan. Unexpectedly, her cousin asked straightaway why she had come to his father's house. She was shaken by the direct question and was not able to reply promptly. Only later did she realize that her cousin was referring to the convention in which married women should only attend her husband's family gatherings. Sipping the tea from her mug, she concluded with a humble smile, "You see what a strange Korean I am."

In São Paulo, as *the strange Korean* she was, Helen refrained from attending most of the events related to Korean families domiciled in São Paulo, explaining that she and her husband had the impression that many at these events looked at them resentfully as both of them communicated in Japanese. Indeed, having in mind the troubled historical relations between Japanese and Koreans in the Asian continent,[3] this may have sounded extremely awkward for those who consider Japan a war perpetrator. On the other hand, Helen did not feel encouraged to speak Korean either, as

---

3.   The relations between Japan and South Korea have been in tension since the end of the nineteenth century when Japan militarily occupied parts of the territory that is now South and North Korea.

everyone in the gatherings chatted in Portuguese and she was still struggling with the language. She conveyed her uneasiness regarding the Koreans living in São Paulo with a powerful image: "It is as if there is a wall between us."

Nevertheless, the ultimate impropriety Helen performed as a *strange* Korean woman was definitively her choice to getting married to a non-Korean. During an interview, she recalled the circumstances of her encounter with her husband and their marriage. She commented that he was some years her junior and in South Korea women usually marry older men. When Helen introduced him to her father, the latter did not approve of her relationship with a foreigner, a non-Korean.

In her accented and paused way of speaking in Portuguese, she stuttered repeatedly: "I think, think . . . ah, I think I will not . . . not be abl . . . I will not be able to get married to, eh, him."

At home, Helen habitually spoke in Japanese with her husband and in Korean with her daughter. Living within many languages, she exhibited recurrent pauses in her speech in Portuguese, signaling the effort to verbalize her thoughts in this new language. What distinguished these moments of stammering from her regular way of making conversation in Portuguese was the intense repetition of parts of the same words. This transmitted an uncanny sense that something more was involved in her thoughts about the difficulties of getting married. I was compelled to consider her marriage as an apprehensive moment that had enduring consequences on her trajectory. This tacit clue made me wonder about how getting married to a non-Korean opened up a whole new horizon of experimentation for Helen, a moment which I will amplify through the poetics of resonance. But before continuing, I share fragments of the conversation that triggered it:[4]

Helen: Uh, how have I met my husband? Uh, I was in Japan, N----- city. He also . . . studied in N----- University. Uh . . . I was studying education, Japanese for foreigners at the Japanese language center in the University . . . For one year, he studied in Tokyo, only Japanese language. Then, he goes to . . . goes to N----- University. He speaks well, he speaks Japanese well. But he . . . was still studying Japanese at the language center in N----- University. I . . . I saw him at the language center, but hummm, but I didn't know, I didn't know him. When there was, uh, a travel, a travel for foreign students . . . we students travelled to . . . an island . . . a small island near N----- city. There, we met . . .

Simone: Ah, that 's interesting. So, you were both students at the center and you met during this travel.

H: Yes, when I saw him, he, uh, smiles. Smile, ahhh, very good-looking. Handsome. But he is younger. Like brother. He, he had an interest in me. He said, he said it later. Yes, I liked him but when I heard his age, oh, brother . . . like younger brother . . . he was not, uh, target, boyfriend target. Because . . . he . . . he younger, uh . . . and he was foreigner too, not Korean.

S: Ah, and for your family, does it matter?

H: When I . . . introduced . . . uh, introduced him, my father, he said . . . I don't like, I don't like foreigners. Brazil . . . it's too too far away. South Korea, Brazil . . . huge contrast. He did not want . . . his daughter, his daughter away. . . . My father went to attend my graduation ceremony. Uh . . . that moment, he met

---

4. The following is an edited transcript of an interview with Helen.

him. My father kept repeating, "I don 't like foreigners, I like Koreans." I think, think . . . I think I will not . . . not be able . . . I will not be able to get married to, eh, him.

S: How long have you been together?

H: Dating . . . I believe for . . . seven years, 2002 until 2009. We, uh, are married couple since . . . uh, 2009, March 2009.

S: Did you get married in Japan?

H: No, in Korea.

S: In Korea . . . Where, in your hometown or in Seoul?

H: It was near Seoul. Eh, would you like to see the pictures?

S: Yes.

H: Wedding pictures.

S: Wow, how beautiful!

H: Traditional wedding.

S: Yes, with all the attires . . . wow, how beautiful, Helen.

H: Everything is Korean.

S: Oh, did his mother attend?

H: His mother and . . . his aunt.

S: Look . . .

H: It's my mother.

S: This is your mother. Oh, my, how gorgeous . . . oh, here is the smile (pointing to a photo in which her husband is smiling)

H: These are my friends. Aunt, friend, Japanese friend, university friend.

S: Is this in Korea?

H: Yes, here is a . . . uh . . . folk village, folk village in Korea.

S: Eh, you got married here . . .

H: Many tourists, tourists. They are all tourists.

S: Look, how beautiful, another outfit. Is this the ceremony?

H: Yes, yes.

S: What a gorgeous ceremony. And everyone attending respectfully.

H: Half attending, half tourists . . . We were living in . . . Japan. We could not practice . . . rehearsal . . . we couldn't . . . my sister booked for us. Later . . . I travelled . . . some months before . . . he, my husband, two weeks before, he arrived.

S: Was everything ready?

H: No, no rehearsal . . .

S: Here, is that you arriving?

H: Yes, yes.

S: Wow, everyone arrives concealed . . . [picture of a handcart]

H: Joseon dynasty in Korea . . . 600 years ago . . .

S: Wow, are you inside? Look, there is a musical band in the front . . . traditional performers . . . Your husband on horse, you inside the box. Were you the one to choose the traditional wedding?

H: I wanted to give him . . . experience of marriage . . . Korean wedding, traditional wedding.

S: How nice, and did he like it?

H: When he commented . . . after the wedding . . . how about his feeling? I don't know, he said . . . he attended an event, not his wedding.

Unquestionably, the interview has a richness of its own, humorously showing the awkwardness of combining a private ceremony at a public historical place; having guests mingled with tourists in the performance of a traditional ritual with a couple was certainly not that traditional. If there is anything that the poetics of resonance can add, it is to echo the uneasiness manifested by

Helen in her stammering recounting of her experience, making us aware of what still reverberates furtively in her personal journey to make a family far from the standards of her kin and homeland.

Smile

Behind the red curtain, the world outside is blurred luminescence and movement. Red light floods the box inside, and the white mantle covering my hands is scarlet tinted. I can hear an old friend, Joon, asking for a cigarette. I sit here, motionless, as if I were sculpted with the *hanbok*[5] and all the little pieces dangling on my headpiece. I am a lonesome princess locked in this little music box. If you could open it now, you would listen to my heart boop-boop-beep-bopping. No one can see me. Yet here inside, immobile, preventing the fake eyelashes, the mascara, the red dots on my face from melting down, I hold this honorable position, head up high, chest upright, hands tied flat. Here I stay, recalling that everything started with a smile. Your smile beyond Korean. Your smile beyond Japanese. Your smile beyond Portuguese. Your smile in the Foreign Languages Center. Your smile in the island. Your smile and the stars . . .

But my father, oh, my father, he did explicitly say in Korean: "I don't like foreigners! You should marry a Korean, I don't want you living so far away in Brazil."

"But, Dad, we're living in Japan! And what can I do if I don't like a Korean? I love him!"

---

5. Traditional formal attire in Korea; general word for both men's and women's formal clothes.

And all the miserable complaints thundering over our heads. Besides the inflaming words already boomed, here we are, my father out there, somewhere, standing with Mom, waiting for us. Here I am, hidden in this palanquin. How far we have come . . . *Where are you?*

I hear drums beating from a distance. The palanquin is being lifted. The guys, my best male friends, are already carrying me. The interior has been shaken and my headpieces are tak-tik-tiking above. My heart pumps wildly. Am I ready? The drums bang louder and slower, the handcart is being lowered. I breathe deeper. The red curtain is being drawn, no other way to flee, it will be the first step on the grounds of our marriage. Tiptoeing the right foot out of the palanquin, finally I see the world again. My eyes search desperately for you. The palace is crowded.

Where are you? *Where on earth are you?*

I see you. I see you in blue. Blue *gwanbok*.[6] You smile.

Indeed, getting married to a non-Korean and, consequently, making a family on the move according to her husband's academic positions across the world entailed an openness that could not rely on customary social scripts. As the *strange Korean* she admitted to be, Helen reflexively elaborated upon such openness by calling it *a different way of thinking*. The first time she used this expression, she enunciated it in English. Later, she asked me for its translation in Portuguese, employing both languages to explain the expression's meaning. For her, a way of thinking was very personally shaped by the situations and experiences one encountered. It follows, then, that a way of thinking could not be inherited or

---

6.   Traditional overcoat for male attire in Korea.

transmitted, and so she, her husband and her daughter, for instance, developed different ways of thinking. People were able to come into similar ways of thinking by being involved in the same circumstances together—as Helen recognized that she and her husband were developing more convergent ways of thinking after being married.

Yet, with this recognition, Helen also feared she might not understand her own daughter, depending on the country where they would be living in the future: "Aahh, baby . . . I believe . . . the most important . . . is the place or country she . . . is raised or lives. I am worried too about when she grows up . . . 15 or 16 years old . . . I cannot, cannot communicate . . . with her . . . her way of thinking . . . maybe will be different . . . she may be able to understand my way of thinking, but she . . . will create, build another."

Their long-term family plans were still unclear at that moment, as her husband was to complete his post-doctoral research at the University of São Paulo and was applying for other academic opportunities abroad. The openness embedded in Helen's notion of a *different way of thinking* was visibly fused with a sense of uncertainty about a future that could not be anticipated, but was within the range of her preoccupations. In the beginning, when they had recently arrived in São Paulo, the couple expected Helen's husband to get a permanent position in a Brazilian university while he advanced his post-doctoral research. Helen became a housewife, taking care of their daughter and postponing the writing of her PhD thesis in Finance. During my fieldwork, Helen´s husband applied for several academic positions at different Brazilian universities, but he unfortunately was not successful. As time passed and the end of his post-doctoral fellowship approached, Helen and her husband's hopes of settling down permanently in Brazil faded away. Her husband began to search for academic opportunities in Japan and other countries in Europe. However, the openness of their *ways of thinking* allowed them to direct their search not in terms of ethnic or national belonging, but in terms of Helen´s husband command of languages at a postgraduate level, such as English, Japanese and Portuguese.

In tandem with the uncertainties of her personal trajectory, Helen's way of thinking was in continuous transformation, incorporating the unexpected events of her life-journey, making it an ever-experimental endeavor without fixed standards of what could or should happen. This process of change also enabled in her a sort of growth of being-in-movement, which she described in one of her Portuguese assignments.

The activity required a written response to the following questions: "When someone leaves her own country of origin, does she lose anything? What? Explain. Does she gain anything in the new country?"

Helen read the question slowly and aloud, making sure she understood it. After pondering for a while, she commented, "One loses, but also gains." Uniting her palms in front her face, moving them forward, and expanding the space between her hands in a gesture of widening her sight.

The following week, she handed in the text below:

One acquires another way of thinking. The person can think about everything in different ways. Therefore, one becomes a wiser person. I believe nothing is lost. However, the opportunity to spend time with friends and family is lost. I do not believe I lost anything. Now I am having the opportunity to live in a different country.

Helen's own vision of herself as a *strange Korean* with a *different way of thinking*, reveals how her trajectory is not a general embodiment of a pattern, at least not the pattern largely pictured in the literature about Koreans living in Brazil. The singularity of her life is characterized by the minute apprehensions and distresses in her peripatetic journey as a wife and a mother on the move. I have sought—responding to her presence as a face— to amplify the implicit textures of her subjective world through the poetics of resonance.

Something Always Happens

Whereas Helen's journey is evidently singular in that she considered it in this way, in this section we follow Mr. Kwon as the interlocutor who apparently, by overemphasizing his national belonging, matches the usual accounts about Koreans living in São Paulo. Mr. Kwon and his family arrived in São Paulo in the 1990s spurred on by his brother-in-law's enthusiasm for new opportunities—this illustrates well what the literature often stresses about Korean migrants being attracted by promising economic circumstances available in cities such as São Paulo or Buenos Aires (Choi 2009, Park 2014). In addition, Mr. Kwon owned businesses entirely dedicated to the Koreans living in the city, particularly those working or residing in Bom Retiro. His businesses could be characterized as integrating the "Korean ethnic enclave" in São Paulo (Chi 2016), where nationals from South Korea are able to maintain Korean as principal language and other cultural habits in their daily routines. Besides these correspondences with the common portrait of Koreans in São Paulo, what I find most meaningful in Mr. Kwon's case is that even while he embraced the expression of a general category of Korean, the imponderabilia composing his life reveal a very singular trajectory that involuntarily subverts general categories.

I first met Mr. Kwon when I found a tiny flower shop in the neighborhood of Bom Retiro with a hand-written advertisement on its window: *Girl who lives in Bom Retiro, Part-time, shop assistant needed.*[7] Walking past cycads, small palm trees, and other leafy vases, I saw a slender man, apparently in his fifties, behind a desk at the back.

As I spoke to him in Portuguese, he squeezed his eyes, slightly surprised that I was interested in the post. In his accented Portuguese, he asked me one-word questions: "Name?"

"Simone."

"Age?"

"36".

"Married?"

"No, but I have a partner."

"Children?"

---

7. Initially, I took the job to pay for possible fieldwork expenses such as travelling to countries abroad, as I was willing to follow some of my interlocutors in their transnational mobility. Later, I realized how my experience with Mr. Kwon actually suited my research purposes. When I asked him and Mrs. Lee about my interest in making my job experience with them a topic in my PhD studies, they were surprised but both said that they would not have time if I would like to make interviews with them, for instance. So, if my period at the restaurant and the flower shop could help me in my studies, they would not oppose, as they considered me to be a student in a learning process.

"No."

"Start tomorrow?"[8] Taken aback by the request, I clarified that I was not prepared to begin so promptly. "Saturday is needed," he added. I proposed Monday at 9:30 and he agreed.

On Monday, the same man was pleased to see me back. He was alone again in the shop and asked me some of the same questions from our first meeting. This time, he maintained a modest smile while speaking: "Name?"

"Simone."

"Married?"

"No, but I live with a partner."

"Where?"

"Três Rios."

"Ah, it´s close . . . Do you have children?"

"No."

"Can you work full-time?"

"No, I can work during the morning."

"I have a restaurant, I need staff for the restaurant. Can you work at night?"

"What time is the night shift?"

"5 to 9."

"I can begin at 5:30."

The job interview ended abruptly and the slender man requested me to follow him. Mr. Kwon never introduced himself to me. He was the *patrão*[9] and, thus, I only ever learned his name through the mentions that

---

8. I tried to maintain in the translation the structure manifested in Portuguese, even though it may sound not totally correct in English.

9. Portuguese: Boss.

other employees made of him. I would always refer to him as *senhor.*[10]

We neared the front door and he switched the lights on and off, remarking, "First, turn on the light." Then he handed me a worn-out broom, detailing that I should begin with the back room and the bathrooms at the rear. This was the place where Mr. Kwon lived. The room comprised a single bed in the middle, a sink and cooker on the right side, and, on the left, a desk heaped with all sorts of papers, a huge flat-screen TV, and a small closed-circuit TV. There were things piled up all over the place: packets of Korean *soju*[11] and soy sauce; empty plastic bottles of water and soft drinks; clothes in a basket; shoes lining the stairs; and shirts hanging from the mezzanine. I began by moving items from their original places and sweeping the floor when I realized I needed a dustpan. When asked about it, Mr. Kwon searched around his place and the storage room. He then demanded that I follow him to a restaurant nearby. We went outdoors, and possibly because of my "Asian"[12] features, he felt free to comment, "Here, there

---

10. Portuguese: Sir.
11. A distilled alcoholic beverage made from rice, potatoes, or other cereals, which is very popular in South Korea.
12. It is tricky to describe people's "phenotypical" characteristics, because this may assume a form of racial categorisation. However, specific body elements were given deliberate attention in some speechless circumstances of my fieldwork. I chose to use the term Asian in quotation marks to refer to people like me, who would be identified as carrying bodily features of people assumed to have been born in a country of the Asian continent, despite this not being the case. I was born in Brazil and

are Paraguayans working, it's no good, but don't say anything."

He then raised the restaurant's iron door. The front area of the restaurant was full of tables and chairs. The lights were off. There were people working at the back, in the kitchen. Mr. Kwon called for a Mrs. Lee and said a "good morning" in Portuguese to the employees, a young man and a petite woman. I assumed they were the Paraguayans I should not make comments about.

He asked them for "that thing to take dirty."

They seemed not to understand the request, so, I tried: "A dustpan."

The young man immediately gave one to Mr. Kwon, who passed it to me. A middle-aged lady arrived and I was introduced to Mrs. Lee, who was the restaurant manager. She and Mr. Kwon kept talking in a foreign language for some time before we went back to the flower shop. While sweeping the floor of the flower shop, I found four coins scattered at different corners of the back room. I returned them to Mr. Kwon, who thanked me with a broad and odd beam. From the gist of his expression, I realized that actually I had been tested. Maybe I did not pass with distinction in the cleaning examination if there were more coins to be found, but certainly, in Mr. Kwon's eyes, I passed the question of honesty and trustworthiness.

When I was finishing the morning shift, he said I was doing a good job and added, "You seem to be Korean." I smiled and thought it was a good opportunity to inquire whether he was from South Korea. He confirmed that he was and asked if I knew Korean food. I

_____

will be considering myself in the account as having an "Asian" physiognomy.

told him I liked *bulgogi*[13] and *kimchi*.[14] He smirked and declared, "You know a lot."

In the night shift at the restaurant, Mr. Kwon greeted everyone in the kitchen in Portuguese and introduced me as *Shimoni*, the new Korean employee. It was interesting to hear my name with another accent, but I felt disconcerted by the statement that I was Korean and awkwardly mumbled that I was born in Brazil and had a father who was born in Japan. For Mr. Kwon, ascribing to me the designation of being Korean was likely a compliment—I had actually been considerably flattered. This revealed his systematic effort to deal with the world by morally judging people according to their nationality. My conduct as a "good" employee had prompted the attribution of me being Korean. Paraguayans, as I experienced in the morning, were regarded by him as not being "good," but it was acceptable to employ them. However, Brazilians, well, Brazilians . . .

Some days later, flower wreaths were ordered and Mr. Kwon requested Mrs. Lee's help. As she was too busy in the restaurant's kitchen, she sent me instead during one of my night shifts. I left the restaurant and found Mr. Kwon in the flower shop working around a wooden base approximately two meters in height. I followed him to the industrial fridges from which he selected the flowers and foliage to be used: white arum, white chrysanthemum, tiny yellow primulas. He asked me to bring the floral foams he had already immersed in water and to peel off the excess leaves from the white

---

13. Popular Korean dish made of thin, marinated slices of beef or pork grilled on a barbecue or on a stove-top griddle.

14. Traditional side dish of salted and fermented vegetables, such as Napa cabbage and Korean radish.

arum stalks. Dried foliage was spread out as background and Mr. Kwon anchored the foam at three different levels on the base. I was instructed by Mr. Kwon to hand him the flowers one by one.

While he inserted them according to his design plans, he asked me in an accented Portuguese, "Brazilian boyfriend?" I confirmed. Mr. Kwon then observed that "Brazilians are all reprobates: they get married, make babies, and leave you alone."

Startled again by another of his statements, I smiled and told him that I did not feel that my partner was a reprobate and there might be good Brazilians, adding that I was Brazilian too. Mr. Kwon did not comment on my response and merely gestured for another chrysanthemum. However, I had a clue about the reasons why he did not highly appreciate Brazilians on the day a girl wanted to apply for the part-time job in the flower shop. The same advertisement I saw was still hanging on the window but Mr. Kwon immediately dismissed her saying that the posts had been already filled. On that occasion, one of my Paraguayan colleagues confided that Mr. Kwon had been sued numerous times by former Brazilian employees for infringing the Brazilian labor regulation, being severely fined by local authorities.

By experiencing the "Korean enclave" through Mr. Kwon's businesses, I was able to see how the "enclave" was in fact sustained in interaction with other groups of nationality living in the city, such as Paraguayans and Brazilians, which induced Mr. Kwon to establish a classificatory system of nationalities that attributed moral standards, on a scale in which Korean-ness would be the most valued one, while Brazilian-ness, the least. Associated with this asymmetrical frame of values, there was an entire informal environment of precarious work nurturing a distrustful and tense atmosphere.

In this environment, jobs were not based on written contracts: everything was agreed orally and without specification; no job duration was usually defined; the first month was considered a try-out period; employees had a day-off during the week according to the businesses demands; there was no mention of social security benefits; and everyone worked both in the restaurant and the flower shop without any specific activity assigned. These conditions generated a work routine continuously punctuated by uncertainty and misunderstandings, and a context full of ambiguity and suspicion at Mr. Kwon's businesses.

My Paraguayan colleagues constantly complained about working overtime and not being paid what they expected, as no record was systematically made and extra hours were never clearly discussed. At times, one of them would feel entitled to have compensation by taking something from the restaurant or the flower shop without Mr. Kwon's permission. For instance, my Paraguayan female colleague in the morning shift had to open her purse every day for Mr. Kwon or Mrs. Lee before leaving, as they suspected she had previously pocketed something that was not disclosed to me by any party. Although this seemed an abusive act performed by the employers, my colleague continued working there for a while. However, every morning she would ask to see Mr. Kwon to claim her due payment and every time she would report that he refused to speak with her. When she realized he would never pay her, she quit the job, as actually she had already been tacitly laid off.

Days later, an anonymous call threatened to snitch on Mr. Kwon's unofficial practices. This kind of occurrence continually pervaded the work routine creating an atmosphere of tension in this informal setting. Not only did the daily work management in the flower shop and the restaurant contribute to this ambience, but apparatuses such as cameras and CCTV monitors were also part of the scene. As already mentioned, in Mr. Kwon's room at the back of the flower shop, there was a CCTV monitor on his desk. The device transmitted live images of the flower shop entrance, the restaurant front door and the restaurant's kitchen. Although I never spotted Mr. Kwon sitting to exclusively watch it, the presence of such equipment made tangible the owner's surveillance concerns.

A sense of work insecurity also emerged from concerns around industrial accidents. One morning, Mr. Kwon assigned me the task of clearing up a corridor at the back of the flower shop where several objects were abandoned. After disposing of cardboard of varying sizes and tidying up an old two-hob cooker and a broken dresser with missing drawers, I came across two large broken glass panels of sizeable weight leaning on the wall. While trying to move them, I inadvertently injured the outer side of my right hand. It did not seem too severe at the moment when it happened; my Paraguayan colleagues were exceptionally supportive and helped me to stop the bleeding and to bandage my hand. I tried continuing working, but my arm started tingling and I could not easily handle any object with my right hand anymore. I informed Mr. Kwon about the accident.

While he could not figure out what happened as he was unable to fully understand my Portuguese, he advised me: "You should go to the health unit." Which I did.

The doctor recommended that I take some time off in order to verify if the tingling would get better or if I should be referred to a specialist. So I was given a five-day leave. Fortunately, I recovered well and went back to work. At the end of the month, when employees were being remunerated, I observed that I received less than I expected.

When I inquired about it with Mr. Kwon, he explained that I did not work during those five days when I was on leave, concluding his argument: "No work, no pay."

Although the conditions in Mr. Kwon's businesses were very uncertain and unfavorable for employees, such work instabilities affected the employers as well. With no formal commitments tying them to work and the low wage offered, many employees worked only for a few weeks, quitting as soon as they could find other better-paid activities. This also impacted on the work routine and required constant rearrangement on a daily basis. The only permanent staff in fact were the employers who were deeply involved not only with management, but also in the preparation of meals and flower arrangements. Both Mr. Kwon and Mrs. Lee cooked, or arranged flowers. Mr. Kwon was more dedicated to the flower shop, whereas Mrs. Lee devoted her attention to the restaurant. They were not a couple, they merely had a professional relationship. Mr. Kwon lived at the back of the flower shop, whereas Mrs. Lee lived upstairs in the restaurant. In any case, Mr. Kwon was considered the boss, who would have the final word on every topic and be responsible for the payroll. In the irregular daily routine in Mr. Kwon's businesses, one employee or another frequently failed to come to work and Mr. Kwon himself would take the job of serving tables or preparing meals. Almost every night in the restaurant, workers would all leave at around 11 p.m. and Mr. Kwon would continue serving customers with Mrs. Lee.

The following morning, gathering the dirty plates and glasses left on the tables, I would ask him what time he had finished working and he would say, "About 2–3 a.m." Mr. Kwon's routine in Bom Retiro was largely absorbed by exhausting work in the restaurant and the flower shop. Once I asked him if he attended any of the many Christian churches in the neighborhood, where many Koreans gathered on Sundays. He raised his eyes from the newspaper he read every day and quickly replied, "I don't have time for this." He added, "I want to go back to South Korea soon."

One of the reasons for his wanting to return was revealed on the same occasion I was helping him with the flower wreaths. I asked if his family were in South Korea and he replied, "I am not married anymore, but my two daughters live there, one is 25 years old, the other, 18." Intrigued by his longing to return to his home country, I inquired how long he had been living in Brazil. He responded, "More than 20 years," while he inserted a flower into the wreath base. Surprised, I could not prevent myself from further questioning why he did not go back earlier. Mr. Kwon demanded another floret and replied, "Something always happens."

Here we begin to observe what is very personal and particular in Mr. Kwon's figure as a Korean in São Paulo. Encouraged to be an entrepreneur in Brazil, things did not go as expected, as often happens in life. Mr. Kwon ended up separating from his wife, and his two daughters grew up away from him, in Seoul. His businesses in Bom Retiro engulfed a great deal of his day-to-day life in such a manner that he has been postponing his return to South Korea for more than 20 years. The instabilities regarding his businesses did not allow him to cultivate religious bonds or enjoy leisure time with friends in golf courses or in other restaurant tables as conventionally depicted (Sampaio 2011, Chi 2016). Meanwhile, amid the inconstancies he has been through, he nurtured a persevering desire to go back to South Korea. Sayad (2006) identifies the idea of retuning as a response to a desire to fill out an absence that is sensed by members in the place of origin; the idea of the return bridges the poles of emigration and immigration, and, among those who migrate, exerts a driving force that sustains values and behaviors for individuals or groups. In the case of Mr. Kwon, the idea of his return to South Korea sustained a justification for him to continue to be "Korean" in São Paulo; it also became his future horizon, towards which he relentlessly turned in order to endure his continuously-delayed permanent departure from Brazil. In this way, he also prolonged his stay in the country as a sort of waiting in hope and precarity (Khosravi 2017).

Mr. Kwon's migrant trajectory expressed in contradictory terms an existence deemed to be temporary, yet lasting more than expected, as "something always happens." "Something always happens" expresses an acknowledgment that life, in the minutiae of the routine of his two businesses, held an open and unpredictable aspect, even though he had a very clear ultimate goal: going back to his country of origin. In the image of Mr. Kwon sitting under the scrutiny of his security cameras, with a silent longing to return to South Korea, the poetics of resonance takes form, called into being by his face, by the singularity of his trials which disrupt the general category of being Korean. Although he might be satisfied to be recognized just as a Korean, I leave the reader the choice to see him in other terms.

Glass

CCTV Monitor 1

Shop window. Her eyes passed quickly on "Girl who lives in Bom Retiro, Part-time, Shop assistant needed." White orchids, red gerberas, a flower shop. She was just passing by. *Oh, why not?* She straightened herself and stepped in.

CCTV Monitor 2

Inside, she passed by buckets of anthurium and silver-leaf, along with mother-in-law's tongue in vases. *Give me luck, Saint George!*

Beyond the refrigerators, a slender man reads a newspaper in Korean. Moments later: "Shimoni, fill buckets with the flower buds! No, not like this. Yes, this way. Half more, please. Nívea will show, Nívea knows. You fill twenty buckets, go. Twenty. I will arrive with flowers, they will need buckets, right."

CCTV Monitor 3

At the back of the flower shop: a single bed, a sink, a gas stove, packs of mineral water bottles stacked, dozens of empty mineral water bottles all over the place. On the floor, behind the door, under the stairs, lots of papers were scattered around in a strange alphabet. *What a shithole! How someone can live like this?*

She swept the floor quietly as she watched, on CCTV monitor 2, Mr. Kwon reading the newspaper: "Anyonhaseyo! Mwol dowa durilkayo? Choropsik kkottabarul chajuseyo? Huh. Chohigage esodo heyo. Otton kkochul choahaseyo? Opsuseyo? Kurom chohihante makkyo jyuseyo.[15] Shimoni, bring the yellow roses!"

---

15. Korean: Hi! How can I help you? Looking for a graduation bouquet? Yes, we have it in our shop. What kind of flowers do you like? Not sure? Then leave it to us. (I am grateful to Heeya Hyung for helping me with these sentences in romanized Korean).

CCTV Monitor 2

Mr. Kwon ordered the staff to get rid of the spoiled petals of chrysanthemums, the thorns of the pink roses, and the yellowish foliage from the silver leaves the flowers stored in the commercial fridge: "Cut the ends off, return them to the buckets."

"Mira, Simone, no se puede vender flores así . . . mira, que están marchitas, una lástima . . . el Señor Kwon, cómo es tacaño. Los ramos vendidos, pronto les caen los pétalos. Yo no compraría flores aquí. Trabajo aquí hace unos meses, pero a mí tampoco quiero ser marchita como estas flores. En diciembre regreso a Paraguay. Sí me voy, no digas nada al señor."[16]

CCTV Monitor 2

On the floor, the remains of plants, petals of daisy, maidenhair fern and palm leaves were scattered all around. Simone carried a broom, Nívea a dustpan; later, both of them dragged a black garbage bag together outside the store.

"Nívea, do you know what Mr. Kwon said about me the other day? That I wasn't Brazilian. He said it to a customer. I found it strange. Then, he told me that I look like

---

16. Spanish: Look, Simone, you can't sell flowers like this . . . Look how withered they are, a pity . . . Mr. Kwon is so mean. The flowers he sells, the petals are about to fall. I wouldn't buy flowers here. I've been working here for a few months, but I don't want to be withered like these flowers. In December, I will return to Paraguay. Yes, I will, don't say anything to him . . .

a Korean . . . Can you imagine? . . . What? You think I look like a *Guarani*[17]? What is a *Guarani*?"

CCTV Monitor 3

At the back of the store, there were broken glass panels about 2 meter high leaning against each other. She was cleaning them, removing the dust, the webs, the dead insects.

"Oh shit!" She had cut the side of her right hand and her arm tingled. "What the hell is this doing here?"

"Shimoni, take off that glove, you are ruining the flower. Oh, oh, oh, the rose bud is now broken . . . oh, this is expensive. Take off the glove, no way like this, no way. Cut the white lace, cut it. Make the ribbon. No, no like this. Oh, Nívea, make the ribbon. Shimoni is wearing a glove, no way."

CCTV Monitor 2

Right hand bandaged, Simone asked Nívea to tie her apron behind her.

"Simone, el señor es un miserable. Mira tu mano herida, él debería pagar un médico y vos no deberías trabajar estos días. Ay, nena, es uno sinvergüenza, el señor me debe dos meses de trabajo . . . en serio . . . Necesito la plata para el viaje y nada. Como si él supiera que me voy a Paraguay y no me quiere libre . . . bah, no tengo papeles mismo, me voy cuando me dé ganas."[18]

---

17. One of the largest indigenous groups in Paraguay and the south of Brazil.
18. Spanish: Simone, the man is miserable. Look at your wound, he should pay a doctor and you shouldn't work these days. Hey, darling, he's a prick, he owes me two

CCTV Monitor 1

Outside, it was night. The key in the latch turned. A grocery bag in one hand, Mr. Kwon entered.

CCTV Monitor 2

Inside the store, a lighted lamp, buckets of sunflowers, calla lilies on one side, vases of raffia and mini-palms on the other. Mr. Kwon's shadow rippled along the way.

CCTV Monitor 3

At the back of the flower shop, a TV sound, water boiling in the kettle, a bowl of noodles and the figure of a small man sitting on the bed. On monitor 2, no one. Then, the noise of noodles being ingested.

CCTV Monitor 2

"Shimoni, give me pink freesia, that one. Another one. Nah, that ugly."

"Is this okay, Mr. Kwon?"

"Yes, put it in the middle, the white flower, like this."

"Is it for a burial, Mr. Kwon?"

"No, this is for an inauguration, a new shop. It gives luck. Beautiful, isn't it? Careful with it. Is Shimoni married?"

"Yes, Mr. Kwon."

"With a Brazilian?"

---

months of work . . . Seriously . . . I need the money to travel, but he does not give a damn. Like he knows that I want to travel to Paraguay and doesn't want me to go . . . bah, I don't have papers, I will travel when I want to.

"With a Brazilian."

"Oh, Brazilians are reprobates, they get married, make babies, and leave you alone."

"But, Mr. Kwon, I'm Brazilian too."

"Now leaf, give me the leaf."

"And you, Mr. Kwon, are you married?"

"Not anymore, I have two daughters in Korea."

"Kids?"

"No. How old are your daughters?"

"One is 25 years old, the other, 18. I'm soon returning to South Korea to join them."

CCTV Monitor 2

Right arm in a sling, the broom rotated only in Simone's left hand: "Oh, this doesn't work! It's not working!"

"Simone, hoy no más, señor Kwon paga lo que me debe o no vuelvo más. La Navidad se acerca . . . voy a Paraguay a ver mi família . . . Y vos con esta mano?"[19]

CCTV Monitor 2

Already without an apron, Nívea went to the back. Simone washed the buckets using only her left arm.

CCTV Monitor 3

Mr. Kwon and the newspaper. Nívea stood up, quietly. Newspaper lowered. The girl standing there was holding her hands.

---

19. Spanish: Simone, it's enough, Mr. Kwon pays me for what he owes me or I won't come back anymore. Christmas is approaching . . . I am going to Paraguay to see my family . . . And you, what about your hand?

CCTV Monitor 2

Nívea left suddenly; she collected her bag and shoes, left the slippers, yelled: "Hijo de una puta!"[20], and slammed the entrance door.

"Mr. Kwon, the doctor said my hand will need treatment. If I don't do it right, I might even lose the arm movements. He asked if it was an accident at work. I didn't know how to say it at the time, but I got injured when cleaning the broken glass at the back. Yeah, I'm not managing to do everything. Nívea has left and my hand is like this now."

CCTV Monitor 2

The left hand could not handle it and the vase of *Falaenopolis* orchids fell off on the floor. Mr. Kwon entered furiously and Simone shrunk. After picking up the shards, petals, and lumps of dirt, she picked up her belongings and dragged herself out to the door.

CCTV Monitor 1

On the window: "Girl who lives in Bom Retiro, Part-time, Shop assistant needed."

CCTV Monitor 1

White lilies, sunflowers in a bouquet, red peppers in display. A crash shook the sunflowers, ruined the lilies, and trembled the peppers.

---

20. Spanish: Son-of-a-bitch!

CCTV Monitor 2

A compact brick on the floor. Debris. Broken glass all over the place. The shop window was ruined.

Mr. Kwon came over and paused. *What the hell, who threw this brick?*

Carefully, he removed the remaining panels of glass.

CCTV Monitor 3

Mr. Kwon carried the broken glass pieces to the back and deposited them together with the others leaning against the wall. Fractures.

The juxtaposition of Helen and Mr. Kwon in this chapter showed how, besides them both being born in South Korea, they each developed very singular trajectories shaped by the specificities of their lives and their understandings of what drives their destinies. Beyond the general category of their nationality, their dissimilar life projects placed each in divergent positions. Whereas Helen experienced the tribulations of getting married to a non-Korean and making a family in constant movement worldwide, Mr. Kwon lived the contrarieties of staying in São Paulo in a highly precarious work routine that prevented him from permanently returning to South Korea. The singularity of each trajectory is unveiled in the fine-grained depiction of what it means to live a life not in general terms. I've used the poetics of resonance to accentuate certain circumstances that made me wonder about Helen and Mr. Kwon in different ways. By emphasizing matters of marriage in a transnational context or entrepreneurship under precarious standards, the poetics of resonance relocates Helen and Mr. Kwon as singular positionalities enmeshed in very particular threads of relationships, sensitively lived in unexpected ways.

CHAPTER 3

Life-journeys

After tailoring an ethnographic experiment to respect the faces I encountered in my fieldwork in São Paulo and specifying how singular each of them was, in this chapter I concentrate on detailing how the imponderabilia affecting their lives shaped not only the singularity of their trajectories but also a sense of a continuing life course, which I refer to as a "life-journey." By understanding my interlocutors' trajectories as life-journeys, I draw attention to how the specificities of their positionalities provide the means to solve certain problems in their lives, and manifest their agency within the constraints they endure. To get a tangible sense of what a life-journey means, we start from an interaction with Helen and proceed by following Kitty again, in the aftermath of the latter's pregnancy.

Life and Instability

During a Portuguese class,[1] I asked Helen whether studying Japanese was a choice in her life or a twist of fate. She frowned her forehead and responded that, for her, the question did not make much sense. She spent a few seconds ruminating on it and, reaching an answer, verbally emphasized that fate also included the acts chosen by a person, and that there was no partition between a chosen life and an assigned life.

In her final written response, she stated, "Life is part choice and part fate. I just wanted to study a foreign language, not necessarily Japanese."

As Helen reminds us, uncertainty is part and parcel of life. The lives illuminating this ethnographic experiment expressed, in varying degrees, this inherent instability in life which I called "messiness" in the introduction. Unpredictability is the human constant from which Simmel developed the social form of "the adventurer" and which he suggested was a synthesis "between what we conquer and what is given to us [...] combining the elements of certainty and uncertainty in life" (1971 [1911]): 192–93). Simmel also highlighted that it is precisely the unsteady quality that characterizes the adventurous that makes evident, by disruption, the presence of the "interlocking of life-links," i.e., those "counter-currents, turnings, and knots [that] still, after all, spin forth a continuous thread" (Simmel 1971 [1911]: 188). It is in this way that the lives of the mobile actors I encountered in São Paulo are intelligible in this analysis: their tribulations and experiences integrate

---

1. With Helen, I had the opportunity to use her interviews and the Portuguese lessons I designed for her as materials for this ethnographic work.

their life-journeys as a series of occurrences in each personal course.

For Dewey (2008 [1925]), a succession of occurrences in the life of a being are called "history." Each life-event is at the same time the beginning of one thing and the ending of another, catalyzing motion in existence and making it transitive and experimental. In this dynamic understanding of life as "historical" process, temporality is an intrinsic trait of any occurrence. However, a temporal awareness of the interrelation between the facts of a life is not automatic. This interrelation is disturbed at each moment when a new fact is recognized, leading to the rearrangement of the sequence of a life. Consequently, a life history achieves significance in the uncertainty, contradiction, and incongruity that are experienced in life itself, because it is through the vivid events of joy or suffering, delight or distress, that a life trajectory can be actualized in its own terms. Such occurrences can completely transform the understanding of previous experiences and the prospect of what lies ahead, reminding us that life is also a movement into the unknown and the unexpected.

Dewey conceived of experiences as being "what men do and suffer, what they strive for, love, believe and endure, and also how men act and are acted upon, the ways in which they do suffer, desire and enjoy, see, believe, imagine" (2008 [1925]: 19). Attention to the inconsistencies, contradictions, and ambiguities that make the world a precarious and risky place is necessary for accurate account of the human (Dewey 2008 [1925]). Along the same lines, Jackson proposes an anthropology that recognizes that "our relations with ourselves and with others [including material objects and abstractions] are uncertain, constantly changing, and subject to endless negotiation" (2013: 9).

This study relies on the many experiences of particular mobile actors I was able to engage during fieldwork. Their singularity was revealed in the course of the numerous occurrences shared or lived with me when accompanying each of the participants of this research. I define this aggregation of experiences that gives a sense of continuity and singularity to someone's existence as a life-journey. A life-journey, then, is an expression of the intersubjective relations established between me and a particular person, which provided me the means to identify the singularity of that person. While following on their heels and bouncing over unexplored paths, I realized that personal geographies and senses of belonging or detachment become dependent on specific personal experiences and itineraries

Singularity and Human Capacity

Not only did my interlocutors reflexively emphasize how instability was present in their lives, but their own courses within and beyond the city of São Paulo revealed how each of them, in the face of certain life difficulties, held unexpected capacities to overcome these difficulties, developing very singular trajectories. Here, the singularly human becomes a testimony of the vast possibilities of becoming unique, demonstrating the diversity of human capacities in the world (Nussbaum 1995). As Rapport (2010: 4) suggests, "our nature is a plethora of capacities, an excessiveness, an overriding capacity to be open to the world and go beyond what is made out to be at present."

Regarding the instability characterizing life, Levinas (1967) states that every being and every event have something irreducible, indefinable, and indescribable that is continually out of reach of certain schemes, systems of knowledge or discourses—in this study, something was often inaccessible by the anthropologist along with individual research subject themselves. It is in this space of indeterminacy that potentialities can inform the motion of a life, and life-journeys can be constantly repositioned and transformed. The unknown and the unknowable elements of life offer great instability and uncertainties in someone's existence, but simultaneously they are an incommensurable resource through which the new can be reached by the adventurer (Simmel 1971 [1911]: 194) and life potentialities can be recognized as "human capacities" (Rapport 2010). In order to respect the presence of the irreducible in each life-journey, one needs to prevent oneself from fixing definitions of what person, event, or world are in essentialist and atomistic terms and reserve space for fluctuating and uncompleted attainments in every life-journey.

By combining the attention to instability as generative of human capacities with Dewey's idea of the life history and Simmel's notion of the interlocking of life-links, the life-journeys I followed during fieldwork can gain further density. From now on, a life-journey comprises *the stream of diverse and multiple experiences that a particular person shared with me* during the mentioned period, as well as *the ambiguities, roughness, and inconsistencies involved in her or his daily struggle for life*. As a result, the emphasis is on the aggregated states and occurrences that a person is able to set in motion, keeping in mind the openness and limits of opportunities that, in the end, make one's trajectory so unique. Limits here do not refer to determinism of any sort—they refer to the situatedness of a being-in-the-world (Heidegger 2010 [1953]). As a presence in the world, every being is specifically substantiated and made unique through its course. However, this situatedness is not a confine-ment—though it can become restrictive in certain situ-ations—but is rather a positionality in the world. In this way, a being can be *restricted* by their positionality and *may* suffer pressures of all kinds by occupying a particu-lar position in the world. It lies within people's capacity to either agree with or resist these forces—with all the respective consequences for every such decision.

If, following Levinas, something irreducible is im-plicated in the very process of existing, furnishing the potentialities of making, remaking, transforming, or inventing the course of a life, concomitantly, each life-journey is not able to unfold unendingly. In fact, each life-journey is situated within the possibilities of its own historicity and involvements. This does not mean that radical transformations or the breakup of significant limits are not possible; it means that, depending on the positioning of a person's life-journey, a person will need to spend more or less effort and resources to achieve certain life-goals. Jackson (2005) regards this situated-ness as a "forcefield": he describes it as a "lifeworld," in which "a constellation of both ideas and passions, moral norms and ethical dilemmas, the tried and true as well as the unprecedented, is a field charged with vitality and animated by struggle" (2005: 7).

In the process of making a life-journey, the situated-ness of a person is informed by certain determinants of a forcefield in which she is immersed, conditioning the number or the quality of life possibilities; but each experimental act can also change the configuration of these forces in the social field that acts upon someone. Certainly, this process is not free from tension, disap-pointment, or suffering. Every gesture brings particu-lar consequences, but every gesture is also charged with hopes of achievement and fulfillment. In this way, each act or experience unravels such a specific concatenation of repercussions in a life-journey that each life-course gains a very singular outline. In this processual movement, in this multiple tension between capacity, decision, social forcefield, and outcome, there is no chance of one life-journey being the same as another. A life-journey is always unique. Still, the singularity of a life-journey is not the same as individualism or individuality. Individualism, as the specific historical and cultural conceptualization of the person and self, corresponding to the ideology of Western modernity (Dumont 1986), was not the issue brought to light by the lives I followed. Rather, individuality was the ontological state of each person, characterized by an independent awareness and sentience that was dissimilar from the world and from other people (Rapport 1997b); individuality was something constitutive of the singularity of life-journeys, however not a synonym for it.

Having reached this point, and after following the singular trajectories of Kitty, Helen and Mr. Kwon, it may be more evident that the focus on life-journeys does not refer to "biographies" in its common meaning, since what is portrayed in this anthropological account does not follow the integral development of a person's biological lifetime and only alludes to the ways in which people told me about and lived some of their experiences during the period of fieldwork I spent with each of them. Amit (2011) develops a notion of "life course," referred to as a sense of life cycle, in order to discuss understandings of youth and adulthood. The notion of life-journey developed for this ethnography does not allude specifically to a person's biological lifetime or phase; it addresses the brief period in which I attended to migrants' life experiences and expectations and could see how inconstant and irregular a person's trajectory could be. However, the idea of life-journey finds convergence with the developmental sense of Amit's notion of "life course" in the understanding that someone's existence unfolds into successive states that can imprint subjective transformations onto someone's life trajectory. On the other hand, the notion of life-journey is inclusive of the senses of agency and reflexivity carried out by a concept such as "life-project," defined by Rapport (2003) as "a kind of self-theorizing and self-intensity that affords an individual life a directionality and a force" (Rapport 2003: 34). Yet, the idea of life-journeys goes further in also covering the unstable and unforeseen states in a person's trajectory that can bring change in varied degrees from previous projects and expectations. Moreover, the life story of each person portrayed in this account cannot be deemed as a representation of an ethnic group (Shostak 1983) or a historical society (Elias 1993), given the singularity and irreducibility of each life-journey that was shared with me.

If there is a life story that the life-journeys gathered in this ethnography do share proximity with, it is Esperanza's story (Behar 1993), the "translated woman" whose life near the border between Mexico and the United States was delicately brought into words in her own terms and uniqueness. The "proximity" is not an ethnic or sociological one, it is in fact born out of the similar conditioning of leading a *human* life across the globe. Notwithstanding that the concentration on only one life-journey would be an option for this research effort, the choice to invest in multiple life stories was made, firstly, because it was what fieldwork offered as experience, and secondly, because it brings a different challenge to convey one singularity alongside other singularities. By acknowledging the predicaments of the imponderabilia of actual life, the fundamental element of regard here is the uniqueness of the life-journeys I had the privilege to follow as expressions of the richness of human experiences in an inconstant world.

Kitty's Life-journey: Navigating Instability, Exploring Capacities, and Becoming Singular

After a long silence of some weeks in February 2014, as described in Chapter 1, I finally received a message from Kitty: "Hi, Simone, how are you, do you know any hospital where I can access the medical care to have my baby?" Kitty had decided to have the baby.

It would take almost another month for us to go to the local public health unit, as she had handed in her documents from Paraguay to a Paraguayan lawyer with whom she was acquainted in order to apply for temporary residency in Brazil. I had recommended that she go to a non-governmental organization specializing in supporting migrants in São Paulo free of charge, but she disregarded my advice. By the end of March 2014, Kitty popped up again in a message, finally in possession of her documents from Paraguay.

On a morning, Kitty and I walked to Bom Retiro's health unit at the end of José Paulino Street. At the health unit, Kitty was registered and had to take a pregnancy test again. A clerk informed she would be visited at home during the following days by a health unit community agent in order to be included in Bom Retiro's health unit care. Kitty took the pregnancy test. The strip must have signaled positive for pregnancy, as the nurse told us to wait for the doctor next. The doctor prescribed folic acid pills to support her pregnancy and said that after Kitty was registered in the health system, she would have to go regularly to that unit to have her pregnancy monitored.

After leaving the clinic, I proposed we visit a cyber-café nearby where many job ads for Spanish-speaking people living in the neighborhood were displayed in the window. Kitty responded that she was working at Mr. Kwon's restaurant again and did not need another job for the moment. She had asked the Paraguayan lawyer to talk to Mr. Kwon and Mrs. Lee after they fired her for being pregnant, and they immediately hired her back, as they did not wish to be taken to court again. I was amazed by Kitty's strategic way of reversing her vulnerable position in the restaurant's informal labor environment, playing with the precarious elements of Mr. Kwon's businesses. She mentioned that Mrs. Lee was even indulging her with food, justifying it as being important for the baby. On our way to her home, we stopped at the local supermarket to get supplies for Kitty and I helped her to carry the items, inquiring if she had news from Jimmy. She told me that he continued to refuse to help her. However, she still allowed him to stay in her room when he asked. For example, one Saturday he had been hanging out with friends and very drunkenly phoned her around 5 a.m. and pleaded to sleep in her room and "check if the baby was okay."

In April, I sent a message to Kitty to check whether or not the health unit community agent had visited her. She confirmed that the agent had been to her rented room at the beginning of the month, filled out a form, and provided her with more tests to be done to initiate the pregnancy monitoring. I offered to accompany her if she wanted, but I got no response. I wrote several messages to Kitty later on. As she did not reply to any of them, I inferred that she was confident of taking care of herself. The following months, I realized that her profile had changed again.

She posted the image of a long-haired white kitten with a red ribbon on the top of its head and the status message: "If you try, you do not lose . . . if you lose, it is not the end." This statement indicated that perhaps she was feeling more positive about her life.

Only in June did Kitty contact me again, messaging that she was not working at Mr. Kwon's restaurant anymore. She was already seven months' pregnant and had decided to have the baby in Brazil. In early August, we finally set a meeting. Since she was no longer working at Mr. Kwon's restaurant, I imagined she would be facing difficulties. So, before going to her place, I searched for public programs that could provide her with support. The next day, I found Kitty drying her hair with a towel at her room's door. Her belly was already showing that she was in the eighth month of pregnancy. She was cooking chicken in her room and stirring a casserole. She invited me to sit, rearranging the contents of the desk beside the cooker. There were black bugle beads, flat sequins, and black blouses spread all over the desk. She said she was not working at the moment, but was embroidering women's tops for a low per-piece rate. I asked if she had been seeing Jimmy; she said he had disappeared from her life.

She poured some water on the chicken and smiled: "Now I have a new husband,[2] his name is Juan." Still stirring the contents of the pan, she added, "I cannot live by myself again." Juan worked during the day, but he would be back for lunch, so she was cooking for Juan.

---

2. Although in legal terms neither Jimmy nor Juan were Kitty's husbands, this was the Spanish term—*marido*—she used to refer to them.

I asked her if he was from Paraguay and she confirmed. Was he treating her well? "Juan is 24 years old and has more brains than Jimmy," she boasted and we laughed together.

She said Juan was a hard worker, but they were having problems with past job experiences. Both of them had worked for two months in an *oficina* owned by a Paraguayan fellow. She operated as a *dobladora*[3] whereas Juan, as a *planchador*.[4] However, the owner fled to Paraguay and had not paid any of the employees. They were claiming remuneration from the Brazilian responsible for the order, but the lady said she had nothing to do with the "Paraguayan job negotiations." At that moment, Juan was working as planchador in another passadera. Kitty believed she was not able to find work now because her pregnancy was too evident. She was concerned that they could not earn enough money for both of them, mentioning that they should have paid the room's rent two weeks prior. I asked if her mother knew she was pregnant. She said that she had not talked to her mother for ages; I took this to mean that her mother did not know about her future grandchild. I commented that I had talked to a social worker earlier and Kitty could have support to have the baby, and maybe even make Jimmy legally responsible for the child if she wanted. Kitty replied that she only wanted to know the baby's sex—and she had to leave after lunch to have an anatomy scan. As Juan would be coming home for lunch, I decided to leave.

---

3.   Spanish: employee responsible for folding clothes, after they are ironed, in the garment industry.

4.   Spanish: employee responsible for ironing clothes in the garment industry.

Later that afternoon, I was walking on Prates Street and accidently met her again. She was returning home from the ultrasound scan. I greeted her and asked about the results. She replied, "It´s a little boy."

Kitty gave birth on October 2, 2014, in a public hospital in the eastern zone of São Paulo. She delivered her baby into the world by caesarean section. The baby had to stay in hospital for ten days. She wrote me a message when she was leaving the hospital without her child. Unfortunately, I was extremely ill myself and could not visit or help her at that time. Kitty brought her baby home on October 13, 2014. She was still recovering from surgery and Juan was desperately trying to get a job. On October 30, 2014, Juan called to say that the pair were leaving for Paraguay the next day. They were going to Juan's hometown to stay with his family.

Kitty's life-journey in São Paulo, similar to Mr. Kwon's, moved within an informal environment susceptible to many uncertainties and instabilities. The circumstances of her pregnancy was one of these uncertain moments when she had to make the difficult decision of whether or not to have a baby in Brazil. In approaching this specific instant through the poetics of resonance in a previous chapter, my intention was to emphasize the unclear moments of a person's trajectory that are part of the struggle to make life keep going. In Kitty's case, it was in the very messiness and peculiarity of her own circumstances that she continued finding the means to overcome the difficulties she encountered. Even though she never bragged about being Paraguayan, she recurrently trusted the network of Paraguayans as support in her pursuit of a life in the city, a network through which she was able to find work at Mr. Kwon's restaurant or at passaderas or oficinas. It was also through this network that she could find young nationals from Paraguay to consider as partners, such as Jimmy or Juan. This network of Paraguayans was ambivalent. It could disappoint her, as Jimmy did not take responsibility for her child, and the Paraguayan passadera owner did not pay her for two months' work. But the network could equally provide her solutions, as when the Paraguayan lawyer was able to win back her post in Mr. Kwon's restaurant, or Juan was willing to embrace her and her child to become a family. Within the specificity of her positionality, Kitty found the means to respond to the troubles she endured. All my attempts to "help" her by offering access to official organizations such as the Women's Special Police Office, the non-governmental organizations that supports international migrants in São Paulo, or the city council program for the protection of pregnant women were irrelevant compared to the resourcefulness she was able to invoke in the network of Paraguayans she was immersed in. Nonetheless, many of the difficulties she faced were also related to her trust in this same network. In ambiguous ways, Kitty lived through this sense of being Paraguayan in São Paulo, remarkably reinventing her life-journey.

CHAPTER 4

Becomings

In this chapter we move now to the life-journeys of Julieta and Liu in order to understand how the adoption of the proposed ethnographic attitude emphasizes the presence of the international mobile actors I encountered in São Paulo as subjects in transformation. As a sense of process and continuity in each uncertain mobile trajectory I followed has been consolidated as a life-journey through considering Kitty's case, in this chapter our journey with Julieta and Liu, akin to Kitty, will show this process of personal change through their experiences of pregnancy and childbirth.

In previous chapters, we have been building up how life is something in-the-making. As Heidegger (2010 [1953]) suggests, to be-in-the-world is to be entangled in the world in the sense of being-in-time, in such a way that being is becoming. The notion of becoming— "the plastic power of people and the intricate problematics of how to live alongside, through, and despite the profoundly constraining effects of social, structural, and material forces, which are themselves plastic" (Biehl and Locke 2017:x)—restores the movement embedded in the life-journeys of my interlocutors. In such a movement, life is an ever-progressing endeavor, an undertaking filled with different qualities of temporality, including moments that are not well defined—such as those of silence, stammering, or waiting—that are part of this very process of life-in-the-making. Giving ethnographic attention to these moments reveals what it means to live in motion as life turns out to be a precarious and contingent experience. In concentrating on these fleeting and transitory moments, life in uncertainty becomes an open venture that carries its own stakes and prospects in the puzzling exercise of becoming, when the person herself at times still does not know precisely what is coming. Still, she goes forward, in trepidation, open to the consequences that she cannot completely forecast, as Julieta's and Liu's trajectories will show.

In Our Lady of Urkupiña's hands

On November 30 2013, in the central district of Bela Vista in São Paulo, an auditorium was crammed. Around 250 seats were filled and people were standing up on both edges of the room. The opening session for the Municipal Conference on Public Policies for Immigrants was about to begin. The members of the opening panel who were requested, in Portuguese, to move to the stage included: a representative from the Italian Association in São Paulo; an official from the Municipal Department of Human Rights and Citizenship; and Julieta, member of the Migrant Women's Base Group. Julieta was not present at that moment and anyone willing to represent the Latin American migrants on the panel were invited to step in. Identifying himself as Bolivian, a young man on the front row volunteered. The panel was supposed to recall the outcomes of previous meetings and coordinate a discussion on the internal rules of the current event before the planned activities started, being chaired by another member of the Municipal Department of Human Rights and Citizenship.

The panel chair began by reminding the process that led to that day and what was expected to follow after the conference. Previous meetings called "spontaneous phases" and "mobilizing phases" had already gathered participants and raised topics of interest. The "mobilizing phases" had generated proposals to feed into public policies for immigrants being drafted. The aim for that municipal conference was to consolidate these proposals from the local level to later present them at the national conference and choose the delegates to represent the immigrants living in the municipality of São Paulo at the National Conference on Public Policies for Immigrants.

It had been almost a year since the Workers' Party-affiliated candidate, Fernando Haddad, had been elected mayor of the city of São Paulo. The "participatory governance" announced in his political program was already reaching the organized migrants' groups in the city through these meetings, pushing forward the possibility of leading a national debate on international migration. The other members of the opening panel proceeded by reading parts of the event rules in Portuguese. A group of residents from South Africa complained in English that they were unable to understand the discussion as no English version of the rules was circulated. An English transcript was immediately provided, together with two translators.

Unexpectedly, I spotted Julieta standing up near the stage on the right side of the auditorium. Many participants offered their seats, as she was five months' pregnant, but she politely refused. I believe she was trying to make herself visible to the panel on the stage, but she was not called to join it. I was sitting at the back, far from her and close to the sound-and-light control room.

A representative from a Bolivian association who was in the audience questioned in Portunhol the delegation group's composition, claiming that it should follow the proportion of the different nationalities living in the city. He was concerned that the Latin American community—according to him, the largest of the immigrant communities—would be misrepresented in the delegation for the national conference. A gray-haired lady in the audience suggested in Portuguese that the city of São Paulo should demand a larger number of delegates since it concentrated the largest number of international migrants in the country. The representative from the Arab community, who was also in the audience, in Portuguese, backed both interventions, adding that the Arab community was one of the oldest and the largest immigrant groups in the city.[1] After receiving these public requests, the panel members deliberated on stage

---

1. The last survey carried out by the Federal Police in 2019 found that the city of São Paulo had a population of more than 360,000 immigrants of different nationalities. Among the five largest ones, 75,282 were from Bolívia, 52,284 from Portugal, 27,414 from China, 24,631 from Japan, and 17,128 from Italy. These numbers express the presence of migration flows that occurred more markedly in the 20th century—from countries such as Portugal, Italy, Spain and Japan—as well as more

that the conference rules were purposely tailored so as not to define the different nationalities as such, because then there would be misrepresentation of the migrants who were really participating in the debates, and thus they did not approve a criterion of proportionality by nationality. Concerning the number of delegates for the national conference, the panel chair explained that São Paulo was already the city with the largest number of delegates in the national conference, so all participants should be attentive not to overshadow other cities in the country. For this reason, the claim for enlarging the number of delegates representing the immigrants from São Paulo was not accepted either. No other requests to change the rules of the event were raised, so, in the end, no modification was applied to them.

After discussing the internal rules of that municipal conference, one of the organizers announced in Portuguese that the mayor had already signed the decree to allow immigrants to be part of the municipal councils in the districts with an immigrant population of over 0.5% residents. The elections concerning immigrant representatives for the participatory municipal councils would be held on March 30, 2014. The announcement was applauded and the participants were directed to take part in discussion groups planned for the event on one of the following themes: promoting and ensuring access to social rights and public services; decent work; social inclusion and cultural recognition; and national legislation and migration policy. As the crowd dispersed, I was able to finally reach Julieta and greet her. She was a bit distressed at having arrived late and not having been

---

recent ones—such as China, Bolivia, Haiti and Angola. (Organização Internacional para as Migrações 2019).

able to play her part in the spectacle of migrant movements' politics in São Paulo.

I had met Julieta years before, during the activities
of a cultural heritage project that identified immigrants'
cultural legacies in the district of Bom Retiro. I had
been in the waiting room of one of the major non-
governmental organizations for the support of international migrants in São Paulo when Julieta approached
me. She was also waiting to speak to one of the organization's coordinators; she had just arrived in São Paulo
from Bolivia and was willing to engage with migrants'
social organizations in any way possible. She mentioned
that she was a food science engineer in her thirties and
that she was not finding compatible jobs in São Paulo.
In this first conversation, I incidentally presumed that
love was the reason that had brought her to São Paulo.

She glowed and confirmed, "Indeed, I have just got-
ten married to a Brazilian."

Bolivians have been migrating to São Paulo since
the 1950s, when the first educational and scientific
agreements between Brazil and Bolivia allowed them
to study in universities in the country. However, since
the 1980s, increasing numbers of Bolivians from the re-
gions of La Paz and Cochabamba have been finding
opportunities to work in the garment industry in central districts, such as Bom Retiro, Brás and Pari (Silva
1997). The figures regarding migrants from Bolivia rose
substantially in the 2000s, signaling a migratory South-
South turn in migration patterns to Brazil (Baeninger
2012). Until recently, Bolivians have remained as one
of the major migrant communities in Brazil, still attached to the dynamics of the clothing manufacturing,
but now spreading to other neighborhoods (Souchaud
2012). They now come from other cities such as Oruro
and Potosí, besides La Paz and Cochambamba, which

enlarged the diversity of the linguistic communities of Bolivians in the city (Silva and Mello 2018). As previously seen with other interlocutors, Julieta's trajectory does not entirely coincide with the predominant picture charted by the specialized literature. Still, her personal course is a testimony to the history of migrants' social movements in São Paulo.

As an activist, Julieta became interested in the cultural heritage project I was working on, and after our first encounter at the non-governmental organization, she attended many of the project's public meetings. During these meetings, she would introduce herself as someone affiliated with the Humanist Movement.[2] For her, the project in Bom Retiro converged with many of the Humanist Movement's principles, such as respect for cultural diversity and encouragement for non-violent and non-discriminatory actions. She was already involved in the Humanist Movement in Bolivia and, in fact, had met her Brazilian husband while attending one of its international conferences.

Over the years, her activist trajectory shifted from a general support for convergent campaigns and projects to a specific political position within migrants' social movements in São Paulo. She finally found the particular political claims she would advocate for while pregnant and giving birth to her first child in Brazil. Wanting a natural childbirth in a country where caesarean

---

2. The Humanist Movement emerged in 1969 and has three principles: the human being as a central value, non-violence and non-discrimination. It is present in hundreds of countries in the Americas, Europe, Africa and Asia. Its founder is the Argentinian writer Mario Rodrigues Luis Cobos, better known by his pseudonym Silo.

birth rates are exceptionally high, Julieta perceived this as one of the real challenges migrant women in Brazil had to endure. In deciding to work for migrant women's health and citizenship, not only did she find a unique place to raise specific demands for migrants, but she was also able to question public health policies in São Paulo more incisively. Concurrently, the gendered framework she introduced into the migrants' social movement debates inspired the emergence of a critique of male dominance in migrant households and facilitated more migrants reporting cases of domestic violence, turning quotidian and intimate affairs into politics. To a great extent, Julieta's sense of being Bolivian in São Paulo was tightly bound to this public performance in the social movements' domain.

After the cultural heritage project in Bom Retiro, Julieta and I became closer and our friendship strengthened. When I returned to Brazil to begin fieldwork in 2013, she was already an established personality in the social movements' forum in São Paulo and was gathering supporters and volunteers for the migrant women's claims she was advocating for. Together with young women from Bolivia, Chile, and Peru, and with Brazilian early-career midwives, Julieta collaborated in activities for the Migrant Women's Base Group. The Base Group organized events to raise the awareness of migrant women about their rights to access public health services in São Paulo. The group also participated in meetings convened by non-governmental or public service organizations and joined parades and demonstrations involving the Migrants' National Day and International Women's Day in São Paulo. On such occasions, Julieta would recurrently introduce the Base Group's purposes with the following personal statement in Spanish: "I am Bolivian, a woman, and a mother."

In December 2013, the Base Group organized a meeting at Kantuta Open Market, one of the well-known Sunday meeting places for Latin American-born migrants, particularly those from Bolivia, Peru, and Paraguay. The activity aimed to disseminate leaflets concerning the rights for migrant pregnant women to have access to public health services in the city and to find pregnant women interested in discussing their cases. At about 2 p.m., a group of young women gathered at the center of the Open Market, around the concrete park benches in the middle of the square: a Brazilian journalist, a lawyer born in Bolivia but raised in Brazil, a Brazilian midwife, a Brazilian training to be a midwife, and Julieta. I accompanied Julieta and the lawyer around the square in their effort to hand leaflets to girls and women passing or sitting nearby, raising awareness about the Base Group's activities. A pregnant woman accompanied by her husband and baby son showed interest in discussing her case. We all walked to a public center dedicated to migrants a few blocks away, where the conversation was to take place. The invited couple were from Bolivia, but their son had been born in Brazil. The husband pushed the baby's stroller around the streets, while an assemblage of women surrounded him. A room was provided for the meeting and all the women sat on couches and chairs around the pregnant woman, while her husband was asked to stay with their son outside.

Julieta began the meeting by asking the lady's name, which she whispered shyly. Julieta then introduced the Base Group's purposes, stressing in Spanish, "I am Bolivian and I am pregnant too." At the time, Julieta was pregnant of her second child. She continued by saying that she knew how difficult it was for Bolivian mothers to gain access to the Brazilian health system, though every migrant woman had the right to health care.

The professional midwife then inquired in Portuguese how many months pregnant the lady was and the latter replied in Spanish, "Six months." The midwife questioned further whether the lady was having antenatal care in a health unit, to which the pregnant woman responded in Portunhol, "I was denied medical care, because I did not have proof of address with my name on it." The midwife asked which health unit she had tried to register in. "Elisa Maria", said the lady.

The lawyer stated that no health unit in the Brazilian public service was allowed to deny access to a patient who lacked documents. Oral information was enough for registration. It was agreed that during the week Julieta would phone the health unit manager in Elisa Maria and the professional midwife would try to check another unit close to Elisa Maria. Julieta gave her own phone contacts to the pregnant lady, as the lady declared she did not have a phone contact of her own. In activities such as this one, it was apparent how Julieta engaged her own personal circumstances to promote grassroots militancy together with other members from the Base Group.

Julieta considered being pregnant with her second child a political statement that should fuse her political presence with her own personal experiences. While her first child's birth had been at home, with the support of a midwife friend, now her daughter's godmother, for her second child, Julieta was keen to make use of the public health system in São Paulo to test the viability of the right to opt for natural childbirth in Brazil, as she advocated for it.

I was truly surprised when she invited me to be the godmother of her baby son some time after we met at the Municipal Conference. Her son's godfather would be a cousin living in Bolivia. I warned her that I did not possess any particular talent for raising kids.

Kindly, she reassured me, "I trust you, you will know it when the baby is born."

As a godmother-to-be, I was able to accompany Julieta and her husband during the arrangements for gaining access to natural birth-monitoring in one of the very few public units sufficiently-resourced to facilitate it in São Paulo.

In March 2014, Julieta, her husband, and I traveled across São Paulo to visit the Sapopemba Childbirth Center in the southern part of the city. With three rooms equipped with bathtub, shower, and medical bed, the Childbirth Center was prepared to accommodate up to three deliveries per day. The expectant mother should make an appointment at the unit during her thirty-seventh week of gestation and bring the results of previous medical tests. If the pregnant woman was well and did not show any sign of health risk, she would attend weekly appointments at the unit, the baby's progress would be monitored, and delivery scheduled. As Julieta and her husband were encouraged by the unit's well-equipped conditions, they decided to proceed with the arrangements in the Childbirth Center.

On that day, when we were leaving the place, Julieta took me gently by the arm and exhorted me: "Remember, do not allow any kind of violence to happen to me or the baby during birth." Because she knew the conditions of giving birth in a country such as Brazil and had followed numerous cases of migrant women's deliveries, she was aware of the uncertainties and particularities involved in every birth occasion. It was indeed a great responsibility to assist her in her own child's delivery.

On Good Friday 2014, the day had come: Julieta's husband phoned me at around 4 p.m. and informed me that my godson would be brought into the world that day. Julieta and he picked me up at Vila Prudente subway station and we all rushed by car to the Childbirth Center in Sapopemba. Julieta complained constantly that the car was bouncing too roughly; she was noticeably exasperated with the labor contractions. Luckily, Julieta's midwife friend was able to accompany us too. At the Childbirth Center, Julieta was promptly escorted to a room.

Unexpectedly, she demanded of me: "Do not forget the holy lady."

This meant I had to take the portrait of Our Lady of Urkupiña from her car to the room, which I promptly did, a bit surprised about the religious request. Julieta took off all of her clothes and put on the blue hospital gown. She was directed by the nurse to try the bed, the shower, the bathtub, and the gym ball. In the room, Julieta's husband, Julieta's friend, Our Lady of Urkupiña,[3] and I tried to comfort her, but she kept walking around the room, the shower, and the tub, swearing the pain she felt endlessly: *Carajo!*[4] *Hijo de puta!*[5] *Mierda!*[6] and other Spanish curse words.

The labor period was tense, since Julieta was being closely checked by the Childbirth Center nurse just

---

3. Although mentioning the Our Lady of Urkupiña, along with other human actors, may sound odd, I incorporate the patron saint in this way because it is how Julieta considered the presence of this more-then-human being in the room.

4. Spanish: Fuck!

5. Spanish: Son of a bitch!

6. Spanish: Shit!

in case the delivery presented any sort of complication. An emergency ambulance was on stand-by if she had to be taken to a hospital for more complex procedures. Knowledgeable of the risks involved in giving birth, it was significant that Julieta invoked Our Lady of Urkupiña, patron saint of her hometown, Cochabamba, to secure a safe and non-violent childbirth.

Similar to Kitty, she appealed to the powers of a more-than-human entity, confiding to me in Portunhol during her labor distress: "Now, it's in la Virgen's[7] hands."

It was this trust on Our Lady of Urkupiña during such a highly uncertain moment that inspired my imagination.

Urkupiña

Carajo![8] This pain is killing me! I can't believe it. Ay, *hijito*,[9] have pity on your mother, don't be afraid to come into the world, I'm just out here waiting for you. Ay, *mamita*,[10] *mi Virgen*[11], stay with me, hold my son's hands and bring him guarded in your infinite love. Oh, mierda! Mierda![12] My back, oh, my back! My child, everything is going to be alright, everything is going to be alright. Mom's here. Hold la Virgen's hand and come out. Ay, mamita, you better than anyone knows how

---

7. Spanish: Our Lady.
8. Spanish: Fuck!
9. Spanish: Little child.
10. Spanish: Mommy.
11. Spanish: My holy lady.
12. Spanish: Oh, shit! Shit!

awful labor pain is. Who did you curse when Jesus was being born? Only mothers are able to understand this moment. Not even God knows what it is. If God were a woman . . . Mamita, what is this pain of giving birth to a child? You must have felt pain, you were human before becoming a saint. Please, mamita, take care of my son and have mercy on me. I make my son holy under your grace. Aaahhhh! Hijo de puta![13] No, no, hijito, it's not you. It's this fucking pain! Ay, mamita, you know I have already promised to visit you in *Quillacollo*,[14] please, bring my son alive and well. Aaaay, *puta madre*![15]

A child was being born and a mother was in pain. During labor, Julieta, kept yelling curse words in Spanish every time contractions hit her badly. In her swear words, I located her strength to go through this highly uncertain moment of giving birth to a child, a moment when control of her body was completely taken away and all the risks involved in childbirth were at play. In taking this instant as a starting point for my imagining through a poetics of resonance, I became mindful of the many aspects of Julieta's life that were involved in her particular situation of giving birth to a child in São Paulo: the importance of the event for her position as a feminist activist for migrant women's rights in Brazil; her faith in the powers of Our Lady of Urkupiña; and her apprehension of being away from family members from Bolivia while making a family in São Paulo. Nevertheless, after more than eight hours of labor, at

---

13. Spanish: Son of a bitch.
14. A district in the city of Cochabamba, Bolivia.
15. Spanish: Fucking mother.

2:07 a.m. on April 19, 2014, Julieta finally gave birth to a boy of 51 centimeters in length and 3.45 kilograms in weight. She was completely exhausted.

Julieta's baby son was born well and both of them thankfully went through the whole process free of violence. Whether or not this occurrence was due to Our Lady of Urkupiña's divine powers was not up for discussion; Julieta had promised anyway to pay her respects to her patron saint by visiting her sanctuary during the festive days dedicated to her in Quillacollo. Thus, later that year, in August, Julieta traveled to Bolivia to fulfill her promise, and I was invited to accompany her and her family. By accepting the invitation, I was able to witness how Julieta's religious commitment not only led her to stand for some minutes silently in the church dedicated to the patron saint in the central square of Quillacollo, but also to climb to a sanctuary at Calvario Hill. On a cliff of this hill, where one can be enchanted by the vision of the lowlands spreading along the valley, numerous pilgrims performed reverences to *La Virgen* and chiseled off bits of stone from the pits of black rock formation. Julieta persistently hammered a rock, while the palms of her hands reddened, and after half an hour she parted a piece of around 20 cubic centimeters. She then carried it downhill, praising herself for renovating her bonds with Our Lady of Ukupiña. She could return to São Paulo and continue with her activism in the social movements' domain as a feminist, a practicing Our Lady of Urkupiña devotee, a migrant woman, and a mother.

Maybe It's Not True

While Julieta viewed the birth of her second child as the juncture integrating her activist conviction with her personal experience and, therefore, as a principled and exemplary episode, in Liu's case, pregnancy and childbirth gained very different contours, as we are going to see. Liu[16] was in her late twenties when I met her and she lived with her husband in an apartment beside mine in São Paulo. Her husband was about ten years older than her and acquainted by Koreans living in Bom Retiro. They had a three-year-old son temporarily staying with Liu's mother in China. Liu was born in a village in the northeast part of China.

Chinese migrants first arrived in Brazil in 1812 as workers in experimental tea farming in Rio de Janeiro (Dezem 2005). After this failed attempt, hundreds of Chinese came to live in the country after working in textile industries in countries in Europe along the century. In the 1930s, some began to move to Rio de Janeiro and São Paulo as travelling traders of Chinese products (Guo 2005). However, from the 1970s onwards, Brazil began to receive mounting numbers of Chinese migrants after the Chinese government established consistent policies of international commerce for nationals abroad, with the formation of numerous business associations (To 2009, Freire da Silva 2018). The presence of Chinese

---

16. As with Mr. Kwon, Liu was not at first chosen to be one of my research interlocutors. However, during fieldwork, when I mentioned that I was interested in writing about her life in São Paulo for my PhD studies, she felt so esteemed that on the next day she provided me with copies of her Chinese and Brazilian documents, though I have never asked for them. Clarifying that I would prefer to refer to all research participants by pseudonyms, she reinforced that she would like to help me as much as she can, as I was helping her with her pregnancy and Brazilian papers.

migrants in São Paulo became largely associated with popular and informal markets of Chinese products in central areas of the city (Stenberg 2012, Freire da Silva 2014), with a business model largely based on personal relationships (Hua-Sheng 2008).

Liu's life-journey in São Paulo does not straightforwardly represent the most commonly studied dynamics associated to Chinese migrants in the country. Nevertheless, her personal course was entangled within part of the network of Chinese nationals already established in the city.

I met Liu when I saw the rear area of my apartment being flooded with heavy food smoke because she was cooking outdoors. I was absolutely irritated when I rang her door and found a young woman to whom I could only speak in English and who justified herself: "I´m sorry, I´m pregnant and was hungry, the dumplings were frozen and I had to scald them." Disarmed by her statement, I enquired about how long she has been pregnant. "Ten weeks," she said, seizing the opportunity to ask me, "Where are you from?" After answering that I was born in Brazil and had a father from Japan, she responded, "I'm from mainland China." She had just arrived in São Paulo three months before.

After this first meeting, my partner and I installed a plastic divide at the back of our apartment and I offered Liu my help in case she would like to see a doctor in the Brazilian public health care system—something I was already doing with Kitty. A couple of days later, Liu came to visit me.

While taking a seat in the living room, she proposed, "Honey, my husband and I would be happy to share the wi-fi and pay for half the bill." I was startled at her request, which she sustained: "I need it to call my family in China, it's cheaper, you know."

She even asked for the name of my apartment's wi-fi point in order to check at her home whether it would have a strong or weak signal from her mobile. I provided her the wi-fi name and explained that I had to discuss her offer with my partner. And since he was not at home at that moment, I could only have an answer later that night. Liu became visibly upset and mentioned that we could ring her bell at any time. Still in the living room, after visually confirming that the layout of my apartment was similar to hers, she also asked about the rent as we compared the amount each of us paid to the landlord.

She found rent in São Paulo very expensive, which I agreed, and she further commented, "It's difficult to have a child in a one-bedroom place, don't you think? Aren't you planning to have one?" Embarrassed, I confessed I was not. She then added, "I only want to give birth and leave for a better life for my child." Intrigued, I questioned where she would go. "The United Kingdom," she immediately replied, declaring further, "I'll have my child and get the Brazilian citizenship. I know that it's easy to go there with a Brazilian passport. You know, I lived for ten years in the United States, where I even got a university degree in Education."

I then encouraged her to possibly look for jobs in international schools in the city, where classes are only in English. But certainly to be hired she would need legal residency papers. "Oh, I'll give birth and receive the Brazilian documents," she confidently said. I interrogated her if there were alternatives to get the papers, as I knew that nationals from Bolivia or Paraguay easily got their Brazilian documents. She shook her head and explained, "I consulted with a lawyer and he told me that only through childbirth I can get the Brazilian documents. It's more difficult for Chinese."

After a while, when she was about to leave, I offered her a glass of water or a cup of tea. She said I should not worry about it, but, in fact, she was curious to see our kitchen. When she peeked into it, she was surprised and remarked, "Oh, the cooker is inside . . ."

Very late that night I phoned Liu to say that after talking to my partner we decided that it was too early for us to share any bill with her and her husband.

Having arrived recently and without documents for temporary or permanent residence in Brazil, Liu and her husband were not able to be signatories of any kind of contract in the country. In order to get access to services, they had to find others to be account holders for them—as indirectly she tried to fix with me in the matter of wi-fi. I supposed that the rental agreement for their apartment had a comparable arrangement, as I remember visiting that same apartment many months before when I was new in the building and knocking on all my neighbors' door in order to introduce myself. A middle-aged man used to live in Liu's apartment. At that time, he mentioned he was half-Chinese and half-Korean, and was possibly within Liu's husband's network. The real estate agency had given me a female name of potential European origin as the tenant of that apartment, though. Later, after another request by Liu for another "favor"—to "lend" her and husband a credit card for them to buy cheaper baby layette—I made it clear that I could only assist her with gaining access to the public services she was entitled to, as well as sharing information about public and non-governmental organizations through which she might regularize her and her husband's immigration status. I might have upset her with this attitude until she realized that I could be of help for her prenatal medical appointments, since she did not speak Portuguese and it was rare for staff in health units to speak any foreign language. So, sometime after, by the end of August 2014, she phoned me asking if I could accompany her in a medical appointment in September.

Liu's particular life history and expectations were mostly shared with me when I escorted her to these appointments in the public healthcare system. In the conversations she and I had while walking to the health unity or waiting for an appointment at the unit, we exchanged observations about life in China and Brazil. For instance, she once asked me, "Do you know if people here can buy the houses they live in?"

To this question, I replied that at that moment there was a housing shortage in São Paulo; consequently, the majority of people living in the city did not own their houses and, for this reason, paid expensive rents—as she and I were both experiencing. Real estate owners benefited from the lack of land-use policies and sometimes preferred not to let their properties, speculating that higher real-estate prices would appear on the market. There were also those acquiring properties in São Paulo as investments, not as homes. Moreover, governmental social programs were still insufficient to provide decent housing for everyone in need, and the city held numerous shantytowns and squats. Prompted by this not very cheering scenario, Liu commented that in China farmers were being removed from land used for cultivation, cities were being raised overnight and the country was not producing enough food for its population, importing massive quantities of it. In another occasion, she retold the case in which dozens of children in China had died because of non-edible substances that had been added to powdered milk, concluding that no one in China could rely on its food chain production, as it was managed by corrupted officials. China was constantly depicted by Liu as a place of serious issues.

However, the most disconcerting statement was voiced on the day when I asked why she did not want to live in China anymore, and she raged: "I don't like Chinese people. I don't like to be Chinese. In China, people have to ask permission to live in a certain place, to work, or to be pregnant.[17] People cannot be free in China. If I want to go to Hong Kong, I need to ask permission, while Brazilians have free access. I want to live in Europe, where my children can have a good life."

In a country where everything in life could be excessively restricted, and impressions of unsafe conditions for living abound, someone like Liu could vehemently despise China. Jankowiak (2008) points out how personal choice in China, when drastically restricted by governmental measures, may produce a perception that people are not in control of their lives and, consequently, not living a satisfied existence. Liu's statement seemed to share such a dissatisfaction, which encouraged her and her husband to leave China. Thus, in her endeavor to achieve the "good life," she extricated herself from an esteemed attachment to her country of origin.

Equally, Brazil was not considered to be the country where Liu would find what she called the "good life." One day we were walking back from another medical appointment and she questioned if I could help her to apply for permanent residency in Brazil after her baby was born. I readily agreed and informed her that we should look for information at the Brazilian Federal Police, the administrative organization responsible for

---

17. At the time I followed Liu's trajectory in São Paulo, China's One Child Policy was still operative.

immigration affairs in the country. She also mentioned she wanted to obtain a Brazilian tax payer number.

I considered these requests to be an indication that she intended to stay in Brazil, which she denied immediately: "No, I don't want to stay here. Schools and health care are not good. People have to spend too much money to have good quality education or health care." And she illustrated her statement by saying that a Chinese friend of hers spent a considerable amount of money to maintain her child in a private school, as they considered the public ones in Brazil very problematic.

When we were to cross one of the streets on our way, Liu also pondered: "With my husband's earnings, we could not afford to give good education to our children here." During the time of my fieldwork, her husband was successively employed in businesses owned by other Chinese in Bom Retiro, such as restaurants and a houseware store. Whereas China and Brazil were not seen as ideal nations to offer Liu the "good life," Europe had an incontestable appeal for her dreamlike future. During a conversation while we waited for her to be called by the doctor, I enquired where in the United Kingdom she intended to go.

"Scotland," she responded right away. "We want to go to Glasgow, my children will have good education and health care there, and it's a place full of job opportunities." Bewildered by such certainty, I guessed she or her husband might have known someone who was living there. "Oh, no we don't know anyone in Glasgow. A Chinese lawyer told us everything; it was the same with Brazil. We knew a lawyer in China who said Brazil was a place full of opportunities, and here we are." This lawyer was the one who had assured Liu that she and her husband would be allowed to gain permanent residency in Brazil, once they had a child born in the country.

Liu asked me, "Could I go to UK without a visa if I have a Brazilian passport?" I tried to explain that someone travelling for tourism to the UK with a Brazilian passport did not have to get a visa before arriving there. The tourist visa would be issued by an immigration official at the airport when disembarking at a British destination. However, the border control official would ask many questions and possibly require proof of sufficient resources for staying in the UK as tourist. In case of suspicion that the traveler intended to stay in the country illegally, the official was authorized to reject admission. Liu became suddenly irritated and argued with me: "No, this cannot be true, they cannot deny entry for people who have the right to go there."

Although my reply to her was the accurate condition in which Brazilian citizens were admitted into the UK and some other countries in Europe, Liu maintained her plans.

Liu's sense of "right" and "citizenship" had a particular inflection, bound largely to her striving to not be limited to being Chinese and to living in China. In her search for the good life, which she considered possible only in places such as the United States or the United Kingdom, she was performing a necessary transition in Brazil. For reasons not disclosed to me, the United States was not an option anymore. Thus, having a child on Brazilian territory would mean that she would obtain national rights, such as permanent residency in the country and other Brazilian documents, with particular attention on the Brazilian passport, in order to get to the United Kingdom. This was fundamentally what it meant to Liu to acquire Brazilian citizenship: a legal procedure to provide her and her nuclear family with administrative papers to move on.

Learning Portuguese was not part of Liu's idea of attaining the Brazilian citizenship, as she believed her stay in the country would be short and I was available to accompany her to medical appointments. It turned out to be relevant only when she discovered she had to provide proof of proficiency in the language to apply for Brazilian citizenship.

She asked me, "Do you know if the Portuguese test for foreigners is easy?" I said that the test was new and I did not consider it very easy, as I was also helping a young lady born in South Korea prepare for it. "Some Chinese told me that it's easy to bribe officials and pass the test," Liu continued.

As I could not say anything regarding that information, she was suddenly alarmed: "Maybe it's not true, maybe it's Chinese people lying to me only to get my money!" She grew irritated. "Now I have to learn Portuguese!"

It was precisely this moment of contemptuous doubt in Liu's reaction that I found the poetics of resonance propitious for amplifying her struggling to cope with the unexpected conditions of her plans.

Definitively maybe

Maybe it's not true

Maybe it's not so easy to go to the UK
Maybe borders are impenetrable
Maybe border control is migrant-proof
Maybe border officials are waiting for me
With snarling faces

Maybe it's not true

Maybe the promised land doesn't exist
Maybe it's a delusion for the fool and the desperate
Maybe there is no such a place like Disneyland
Maybe it's just a way to keep walking
With calloused feet

Maybe it's not true

Maybe it's not so easy to live in Brazil
Maybe it's not so simple to get Brazilian citizenship
Maybe the Brazilian passport is not a ticket to the UK
Maybe it's just the desire of having another child
To dream with me

Maybe it's not true

Maybe I won't ever stop being Chinese
Maybe the English I learned is useless
Maybe the doors of the world are already closed
Maybe there only exists cracks on the wall for the
unfortunate
To peek at happiness elsewhere

Maybe it's not true

Maybe the system has already traced my destiny
Maybe good life is the new utopia
Maybe I won't be able to change what the great powers
decided
Maybe all ears will be deaf to my claims to
aspire for the impossible

Maybe

But all the same, I'll try

For Liu and her husband to become Brazilian citizens and get the Brazilian passport, they would have to go through the process of "naturalization." This was the official procedure that allowed foreigners to "become Brazilians." It is highly ambiguous whether Liu and her husband's decision to have a baby in Brazil was entirely pragmatic or was carried out for the joy of parenthood. Possibly, both options were at play at the same time, as they were a young couple. But it was no wonder that Liu's pregnancy in Brazil became a key component in the family's striving for the good life. By the end of my fieldwork, Liu was about to give birth. Before I left São Paulo, she asked me to show her the nearest notary office where she could register her baby as Brazilian. She was thrilled that that moment was imminent. After delivery, she planned to go back to China to introduce her baby to her extended family and bring her eldest son to Brazil. Her nuclear family would then be finally complete.

Liu's life-journey was undeniably directed towards searching for a good life for her family. In this quest, she developed an acute critique about the country she had been born in and other places that could not offer the necessary conditions to provide the well-being she expected. No national border or identity was substantial enough to prevent her from trying to achieve her goal. She did not hold being Chinese in high esteem; she did not appreciate it, but at the same time she did not envisage herself personifying any other specific nationality. For her, nationalities seemed to be a matter of legal performance that were worth attaining only when they allowed her to reach the "good life." She considered nationalities mostly through the bureaucracy of citizenship. Her first attempt to have a good life in the United States was interrupted by something she did not reveal to me. During her stay there, she had been proud of herself for getting a higher education degree in an American university. Not pleased to go back to China, she and her husband came up with another possibility: getting another nationality that would allow them to access another English-speaking nation in which a good life would be possible: the United Kingdom. This is how Brazil became included in their plans. Brazil was the place where they would be able to reformulate their lives and nationalities in order to have the chance of a desired life in another country. The key element to this strategy was giving birth to a child on Brazilian soil.

CHAPTER 5

Immensity

The life-journeys portrayed in the previous chapters are evidence of the richness embedded in a migrant's existence: these trajectories show how singular each life-journey becomes in its own unfolding. They are characterized by uncertainty, undefined but significant moments, and particulars that allow us to understand these actors as singular presences in a field of relations which they navigate, change and are changed by. This ethnographic exercise has involved a poetics of resonance to amplify those often unspoken and overlooked moments of uncertainty in evocative ways and the conception of my interlocutors' lives as a continuing process of subjective transformation through the notion of life-journey. Correspondingly, by amplifying some moments of silence, stammering, waiting, pain, and rage in Kitty's, Helen's, Mr. Kwon's, Julieta's, and Liu's trajectories through a poetics of resonance, we can sense how fragile life is. In this chapter, I discuss some impacts for migration and urban studies resulting from the approach here, such as the decentering of dominant categories of ethnicity and nationality, and the possibility of considering migrants' lives through the concept of immensity.

Decentering Ethnicity and Nationality

The lens of life journeys emphasizes the processual and contradictory evolvement of a migrant's trajectory in São Paulo and abroad, and repositions the significance of ethnicity and nationality vis-à-vis other sorts of categories, such as class, gender, age, or citizenship, to cite a few. In this manner, it converges with the effort for "de-essentializing ethnicity" (Bauman and Sunier 1995: 1), considering it entangled with other aspects that are subsumed in a person's singular positionality. This does not mean that ethnicity and nationality do not play important roles in the lives of migrants. It means that ethnicity and nationality should be considered critically without supposing, for example, that they inevitably lead to gestures of "social cohesion" and "collective commitment" (Bauman and Sunier 1995: 4). Mr. Kwon's and Kitty's life-journeys revealed that senses of national belonging can work as chief references in everyday life. For instance, Mr. Kwon reinvented himself as a Korean living in a country he did not feel was his. Meanwhile cultivating a longing for returning to South Korea, he organized businesses aimed exclusively at Korean customers in São Paulo and avowed Korean nationality to be a primary orientation to morally judge people and the world. Similarly, Kitty trusted a network of Paraguayans living in the city, through which she was able to find job opportunities, regularize her permanency in Brazil, and have love affairs. Whereas Mr. Kwon emphasized a sense of being Korean in extreme contrast with other nationalities, Kitty's sense of being Paraguayan was performed by not regarding any other nationality as a reference to direct her life. While Mr. Kwon persistently pursued being Korean, Kitty quietly subscribed to being Paraguayan. Yet both of them, in the dynamics of their routines, went through disappointing experiences by relying on national affiliation as central reference for their life-journeys in São Paulo.

Mr. Kwon enlivened a sense of being Korean while sustaining a precarious labor environment that prevented him from returning to his beloved country of origin, as "something always happened." Kitty's trust in her Paraguayan network led to her relationship with Jimmy and her pregnancy, but not to the security of shared parenthood; it led to a job in a passadera but not secure payment. Contrary to Durkheimian understandings (Durkheim 2014 [1893] and 1995 [1912]) that senses of belonging emanate from collective forms of organization and reinforce these very communal bonds, Mr. Kwon and Kitty instead had life-journeys whereby senses of ethnicity and nationality offered disintegrating outcomes for each of them. During his stay in São Paulo, Mr. Kwon saw his family come apart and was bound in a working routine that did not give him time to create religious bonds or share leisure moments. Likewise, Kitty suffered intimate abandonment and unpaid work by trusting a Paraguayan network established in the city.

Life-journeys show how ethnic and national categories of belonging are precarious and contradictory, and don't hold the coherence and rationality that is often attributed to them. In accepting the instabilities and inconsistencies of ethnic and national references in everyday life, life-journeys, as a methodology, draw attention to how the minutiae of someone's ordinary struggle through the inconsistencies of the world constantly disrupts stable concepts of ethnicity. As the poetics of resonance made apparent, within a life-journey, there are particulars that do not compose a coherent and intelligible explanation of someone's life; rather, they are part of a life-journey and they can be lived as occurrences in which the person and the world are put in question or on hold. In the life-journeys portrayed in this account, life was also trial and error, not an abstract model. The senses of being Korean and Paraguayan in the life-journeys of Mr. Kwon and Kitty show that ethnic-cum-national[1] affiliations represent "an emic category of ascription" (Eriksen 2010: 16). However, as the life-journeys of Mr. Kwon and Kitty indicated, nationalities or ethnicities can offer a starting point to support the making of a life, but they are not sufficient in themselves, as life overflows them.

Another aspect in the operation of de-essentializing certain categories of analysis that the life-journeys as an approach also stimulates is the interest in understanding migrants' lives beyond the boundaries of the nation-state. Concurring with scholarship from transnational migration studies, I consider migrants' trajectories in the "simultaneity" of their social ties and beliefs of belonging by acknowledging that "persons can engage simultaneously in more than one nation-state and a nation-state does not delimit the boundaries of meaningful social relations" (Levitt and Glick Schiller 2004). Their presence thus become a "step toward dis-ordering the conventions of state-hood" (Hyndman 2000: xx). Julieta's and Helen's life-journeys certainly

---

1. Nationality and ethnicity have been dominant categories in migration studies and at times overlapped into one another. I use the expression "nationality-cum-ethnicity" to refer to their usage separately or combined.

show more emphatically how such simultaneity embeds migrants' everyday lives and provides senses of multiple belonging. Julieta articulated a sense of being Bolivian in intimate dialogue with her activism in social movements and her own familial project in São Paulo, an identity mediated too by her religious bonds with Our Lady of Urkupiña. She conceived herself as a Bolivian in São Paulo by taking seriously her experiences as a migrant woman and a mother. Unlike Mr. Kwon, she did not categorize her national affiliation as being morally "better" than other nationalities, but she asserted being only Bolivian and at times considered returning to her country of origin. In contrast, Helen felt she was not a "proper" Korean very early in her life, but getting married to a non-Korean became her ultimate feat in being a "different" Korean. Although she missed her family from South Korea, having a nuclear family and raising children across the world were the principal motives driving her international trajectory, which was composed by the different academic affiliations her husband found. For this reason, Helen was not very attached to a Korean identity and did not attend many of the events associated with Korean families living in São Paulo. In a similar fashion, while Liu did not highly praise being Chinese, paradoxically her main reference for managing a life in São Paulo revolved around a network of Chinese who connected diverse cities and countries in the world, and were reasonably-informed about the different regulatory regimes ruling different national citizenships. In focusing on such individual trajectories, the approach through life-journeys shows how the multiple networks established by each migrant between different nation-states are tangibly arranged and experienced. It emphasizes how such constellations of networks are transient and changeable according to specific social circumstances and the capabilities that each migrant is able to activate or de-activate in a definite period of time.

By emphasizing the transitory aspect in the experience of the international migrants I came to encounter in São Paulo, the approach of life-journeys accords with the attention to the movement—physical, social and existential—ingrained in the everyday life of migrants as proposed by the paradigm of mobility studies (Cresswell 2006, Sheller and Urry 2006 and Urry 2007). More particularly, regarding migration studies, mobility studies consider "the myriad ways in which people and their cultural practices are not confined to a fixed territory but are part of multiple spatial networks and temporal linkages" (Glick Schiller and Salazar 2013: 185-86), opening up possibilities for analysis to integrate geographic mobility and social mobility while challenging analysts to not lose sight of the specific grounds of each milieu when adopting the framework of a comprehensive concept such as mobility (Brettell 2018).

The Singular, the Personal and the Unexpected

The life-journeys approach relocates the significance of ethnicity and nation-states in a migrant's trajectory and highlights the importance of the personal and the subjective by insisting on considering the role of individual agency and perception in migration studies (Amit-Talai 1995). Rather than departing from general categories of belonging and membership outside our interlocutors' worlds, it privileges migrants' own categories of identity and affiliation to reach a more complex understanding of their lives in their own terms. In this way, we are able to appreciate how Kitty, Mr. Kwon, Helen, Julieta, and Liu performed senses of belonging and self in very unique ways.

Mr. Kwon developed a very particular way to be Korean in São Paulo by grounding his businesses to serve the Korean community in the city in activities that are usually ascribed to women: cooking and arranging flowers. He did not have a nuclear family or relatives in Brazil and did not spend time in any of the Christian churches of the Korean community in the city, as some descriptions of Korean men living in São Paulo portray (Sampaio 2011 and Chi 2016a). On the other hand, Kitty enunciated her sense of belonging by discreetly participating in the informal network of Paraguayans living in São Paulo. In this, she could find casual work at outsourced businesses such as Mr. Kwon's restaurant or passaderas, as well as boyfriends or partners of Paraguayan origin. These particular renderings of membership emphasize how an individual expresses a sense of identification to a nation in very personal ways, whereby "the nation is one of the resources on which individuals draw to formulate a sense of selfhood" (Cohen 1996: 803).

In this line, but with more national dimensions overlapping one another, Julieta developed a pendular migratory movement between Brazil and Bolivia related to her attachments to her nuclear family in São Paulo, her position in the migrants' social movements, and her commitment to popular practices of Catholicism in Bolivia. Thus, she regarded herself a Bolivian who was born in Quillacollo; was a devotee of Our Lady of Urkupiña; and had significant experiences concerning Brazil, such as having married a Brazilian, raising her children in Brazil, and advocating for female migrants' rights in São Paulo. This multifaceted character of transnational belonging found in the discursive practices of many migrants can be framed as being "tensile" (Rapport 2012b). The tensions involved in such a personal rendering of belonging show that this sort of enunciation is not uniform, but situationally operated within an array of additional ways of being. In Julieta's case, one is "Bolivian" in tension with being a "mother," a "patron saint devotee," an "activist," and so on. In taking into account how each person construes a sense of belonging in her or his own terms, it is possible to appreciate how life is authored in such a way as to navigate the complexities involved in it.

Comparably, Helen's life-journey and musings about not fitting properly a specific national category express more incisively this complexity involving a personal engagement with matters of belonging. Helen developed an ironic reflexivity (Rapport 1997b) through which she questioned conventional values and repositioned herself by opening up possibilities to create novel meanings that allowed her to advance in the world in her own terms. In her unique journey to understand herself and to live a life beyond a national category with which she did not feel comfortable, Helen conveyed an alternative understanding of herself by devising the notion of "ways of thinking." According to Helen, a way of thinking emerges from the particular situations and experiences a person goes through. In this view, no one is able to transmit a way of thinking to another person. Each way of thinking is unique for the mere reason that it is impossible for anyone to have exactly the same experiences as another. Helen, for example, was afraid of not understanding her own daughter in the future, because her daughter would develop a totally different way of thinking when growing up in a different setting with different experiences. Helen's idea of a way of thinking is a self-authored path to overcome the uneasiness of not properly suiting the categories she or any member of her family was supposed to fit into. It offered an openness to becoming something else in her own terms, beyond the restricted vocabulary of nationality-cum-ethnic terms. This openness in Helen's life-journey, as a capability, created other parameters through which to reason about her particular worldwide trajectory, accompanying her family.

In a similar fashion, Liu did not subscribe to belonging to the nationality of the country she was born. More radically, she abhorred it in a perplexing version of an ironic attitude that enabled her to develop a critical stance regarding categories of nationality. As with Helen, this reflexive attitude also allowed Liu to conceive of the world in her own terms, by fostering the idea of the "good life" as a guiding force to accomplish a will to live in a nation of consolidated welfare structures. In pursuing the good life, Liu perceived nationalities only as a matter of legal performance, worked out mostly as "bureaucratic citizenships." Consequently, her sense of right and citizenship was largely bound to her goal of not being limited to being Chinese and living in China, as well as not being significantly attached to Brazil or to a Brazilian identity. More akin to what Ong (1999) called "flexible citizenship," Liu responded fluidly and opportunistically to the political-economic conditions the world offered to her, navigating the rationalities of nation-states and family-making in very peculiar ways. In refusing to assert nationality as a defining feature of her belonging, Liu affirmed a sort of distinct prerogative of humanness that would exist beyond categorizations of nationality in her search for the good life. This distinct sense of humanness was expressed by Liu in her maneuver to empty nation-state expedients, such as citizenship documents issued by national authorities, of a significant sentiment of national belonging. Her maneuver explicitly turned nation-state rights and citizenship into bureaucratic procedures, but implicitly made manifest a demand for an entitlement to access the wellbeing available only for a restricted part of the world's population.

Moreover, the focus on the singular and the personal in each life-journey also brought to the fore the precarious and unstable dimensions embedding the imponderabilia and messiness of each particular course, which were emphatically acknowledged and expanded by the use of the poetics of resonance. In revealing the minutiae involved in the making of Kitty's, Helen's, Mr. Kwon's, Julieta's, and Liu's life-journeys, a sense of instability became overly apparent in the constitution of their worlds. Correspondingly, many of the situations described in this ethnographic experiment are evocative of occurrences and circumstances portrayed in studies about refugees and war displacement in migration studies. Hence, the evidence sustained by the life-journeys of Kitty, Helen, Mr. Kwon, Julieta, and Liu converses on a certain level with the "ethnographies of uncertainty" (Cooper and Pratten 2015) and "chaos" (Lubkeman 2008) regarding the unstable and bewildering situations of war and its related displacements as well as the accounts on the "precarious lives" of youth worldwide (Khosravi 2017, Daalsgard et al. 2014). It concurs in indicating that uncertainty is also a productive element generating new social horizons and social landscapes populated by "subjunctive subjectivities" whose "modes of comportment and practical strategies" give expression to "micro-sociologies" of "open-ended relationships" (Cooper and Pratten 2015: 13). Furthermore, uncertainty can equally be seen as an asset in my research participants' life-journeys too, a "resource that permitted them to hope in ways that they could not in less uncertain situations" (Turner 2015: 190). In such uncertain scenarios, they made use of the "small things and events" regarded as micro-tactics of waiting and hope (Khosravi 2017:20), whereby "the experience of time" becomes "an often-troubling, external factor in life, as well as the concomitant emotional unrest and the perhaps innovative acts motivated by it" (Dalsggard et al. 2014:1). Despite my interlocutors not living under conditions of armed conflict and related displacement, such as the drama of Machazian war-time existence in Mozambique, "centered on the pursuit of a complex and multidimensional agenda of social struggles, inter-personal negotiations, and life projects" (Lubkemann 2008: 14), their lives coincide with the disrupting but fecund significance of instability in everyday social life. The uncertainties associated with Kitty's, Helen's, Mr. Kwon's, Julieta's, and Liu's life-journeys, by not being permeated by issues of warfare, emphasize what Butler (2004 and 2010) defines as "precariousness," a common human condition of being vulnerable before others in the world, as introduced in the first pages of this book.

Complexity

As a consequence of an approach that is not centered on categories of ethnicity or the boundaries of nation-states, diversity is then manifested in the singularity of each personal rendering of difference in a life-journey. Diversity here gains other possibilities of actualization in expressions such as richness, thickness, or density, as the minutiae involved in the making of each life-journey engender a variant sense of complexity. This sense of complexity is dissimilar from usual notions of complexity applied in migration studies, which are generally grounded in forms of ethnic and social classification associated with nation-state-led references, as portrayed in some of the works discussed below. Complexity for these latter is discussed in terms of multiplicity of categories or sets of categories, for instance in debates on multiculturalism or migrants' multiple identities, as migrants are generally conceived of in relation to an original nation-state and a host nation-state .

In this framework, considerations on migrants and multiculturalism are largely conducted around concepts such as "culture," "integration," "minority," "majority," and "community," which then revolve back to the scale of the nation-state. Studies in this line of scholarship analyze, for instance, discourses conveyed by ethnic groups living in certain areas of global cities that intentionally reify terms such as "community" and "culture" as a way to affirm collective identities whereby one can observe "communities within communities, as well as cultures across communities" (Bauman 1996: 10). In issues of integration, work has been also exploring the "criteria of exclusion and inclusion in a given social environment" (Eriksen 2007: 1060) by refining notions of "majority" and "minority" so as to identify degrees of "openness" and "closedness" that accommodate collective processes of hybridity and fragmentation in the pluralistic societies of the contemporary world. In a similar vein, another strand of analyses, by recognizing that the concept of ethnicity is not sufficient to give a full account of migrants' presence in multi-ethnic contexts, incorporates other dimensions of migrants' statuses such as "entitlements and restrictions of rights, divergent labor market experiences, discrete gender and age profiles, patterns of spatial distribution, and mixed local area responses by service providers and residents"

(Vertovec 2010: 67) to reach a multidimensional understanding of an ethnic collective by means of the concept of "super-diversity." In common, these approaches propose new research agendas by "fragmenting" or "multiplying" the categories of community, culture, society, or other related terms in migration studies.

Similarly but in a slightly different manner, the debate about migrants' multiple identities also reinforces an understanding of complexity based on forms of ethnic and nation-state-led categorizations. For example, Bhachu (1985) defines the East African Sikh immigrants living in Britain as "twice migrants." In describing the network of elements linking the Asian groups in East Africa and the East African Sikh living in the United Kingdom, the author discloses how these groups employed practices of marriage and dowry as a means to activate processes of adaptation, continuity, and change. The multiple identities conveyed in this work refer to the different continental locations lived subsequently by an ethnic group and their efforts to maintain a rationale as a group through time and generations. Correspondently, Basch et al. (1994) suggest that the identity of transnational migrants is shaped through constructions of race and ethnicity simultaneously conducted both in their home country and their host country. In many ways, the multiplicity of identities of transnational migrants would also be attached to figurations of citizenship, in which processes of hegemony and subordination demarcate the manifestation of such identities. In these accounts of migrants' multiple identities, subjects become multiple according to the number of engagements with the different categorical dimensions of the nation-state. A migrant's identity, then, is understood as an "accumulation" of all the state and ethnic categories to which one is related. By not working with ethnic and national sorts of categorizations and not "fragmenting," "multiplying," or "accumulating" such categories, the life-journeys approach aims to comprehend complexity in the dense observation of contradictory and incomplete modes of making and/or unmaking migrants' subjectivities. It emphasizes ambiguous dimensions of identity and forms of belonging.

This complexity thus does not refer either to the flow of cultural meanings collectively shared and publicly juxtaposed, merged, or creolized in the interconnectedness of the "global ecumene" as Hannerz (1996) characterizes it. The complexity in the approach through life-journeys rather coincides with the "unexpected and unstable aspects of global interactions" (Tsing 2005: 3), which open uncertain but creative "zones of awkward engagement," where incomprehensibility and indeterminacy become part of such a system of "odd connections" (Tsing 2005: xi). It becomes more evident that the complexity elicited by the life-journeys of Kitty, Mr. Kwon, Helen, Julieta, and Liu does not refer to a notion of culture as the organization of meaning as Hannerz (1996) has it. Rather, the life-journeys, through the support of a poetics of resonance, revealed that life is also made up of gaps and moments of suspended meanings. Here, shared meaning is challenged by the precarious and uncertain situations lived through people's life-journeys. Moments of incomprehension and perplexity are thus part of people's life flow and misunderstanding and opacity become components of their lives' complexity. Thus, neither nuanced elaborations based on categorizations of diversity nor systems of shared cultural meaning reflect the complexity enlivened by the approach through life-journeys.

The complexity resonantly evoked through the life-journeys of Kitty, Mr. Kwon, Helen, Julieta, and Liu

has thus aimed to be the expression of the "uniqueness" of their human experiences, following Levinas's
(1987, 1998) terms. In attempting to reach this, Kitty,
Mr. Kwon, Helen, Julieta, and Liu could be deemed to
be subjects whose lives were so rich and dense that no
categorization would ever be sufficient to define their
beings. Since it is not possible to achieve an explication
of the totality of their existences, mystery will always be
part of the complexity that entails their lives. In respecting this mystery, the recourse to a poetics of resonance
and the notion of life-journeys allows only a glimpse
into their respective experiences, valuing the potentialities of what each of them may hold and become. Within
the complexity of their personal circumstances, Kitty,
Mr. Kwon, Helen, Julieta, and Liu found their own ways
to carry on with their lives.

"Going beyond": An Alternative to Categorization Thinking

Migrants have often been defined by the application
of certain categories of classification. Concepts such as
nationality, citizenship, ethnicity, class, gender, religion,
or age became usual components in this proceeding. As
a result, categorization in migration studies has been
a significant operation in many methodological approaches. For instance, a usual way to engage with Mr.
Kwon's and Helen's stories in migration studies would
be by grouping them as South Korean migrants; or to
portray Kitty as a representative case of Paraguayan labor migrants in Brazil.

In refusing to reduce the research participants of
this account to categories—as Levinas (1967) advised—and choosing not to apply such operations of

classification by adopting a cosmopolitan (Rapport 2010) and an existential approach (Jackson 2013), the core intention of my ethnographic work is to portray Kitty, Mr. Kwon, Helen, Julieta, and Liu as people whose particular existences can be testimonies of genuine ways to be singularly human. This approach appreciates the conditions of existence as a transient and incongruous experience, in which trivial facts disclose how life is never lived in general terms. As Jackson maintains: "We must go with the broken flow of migrant narratives and migrant imaginaries, working out ways of doing justice to the often paratactic, contradictory, opportunistic, and improvisatory character of transitional experience" (2013: 8). The mundane, the minute and the unanticipated of the everyday practices of specific migrant lives are opportunities to acknowledge the complexity involved in the making of life itself.

In taking into account the irreducibility of any research subject to social or cultural categories by privileging the singularity of each person's life-journey, this book provides a glimpse into migrant lives and their quotidian efforts to lead a life, decentering classifications of nationality, ethnicity, or citizenship as core references. Concomitantly, this book has been concerned with the associated operation of essentializing migrants under such classificatory standards, being cautious not to enact what Hyndman calls, in the case of refugees, a "semio-violence," a representational practice that effaces our interlocutor's voices by dematerializing them in the general taxonomies and statistics of scholarly accounts (2000:xxii). It is my hope that this ethnography might have offered brief insights into Kitty, Mr. Kwon, Helen, Julieta, and Liu as presences in the richness of their complexity and mystery. In this way, the category of migrant could be overcome in favor of appreciating these lives not as objectified generalizations but as particular dramas in the struggle to exist in the world. Kitty, Mr. Kwon, Helen, Julieta, and Liu operated with notions of nationality, ethnicity, gender, kinship, or citizenship. However, to encapsulate each of them under such generalist terms would be to subdue some of the complexities and potentialities depicted in the previous chapters.

In fact, the approach through life-journeys proposes an alternative to categorization thinking in migration studies much in line with what Rapport (2010) called a "going beyond": "to go beyond the categorical features of symbolic classifications—the boundaries between things and relations—that human beings at the same time invent so adeptly and defend so vehemently" (2010: 3). By methodologically "going beyond" categorization thinking in migration studies, the life-journeys' approach unlocks the possibility to substantively explore the fluidities and complexities inherent in the worlds of the "people who live their lives in movement [and] make sense of their lives as movement" (Rapport and Dawson 1994: 7).

From Identity to Immensity

The approach of the poetics of resonance and life-journeys thus uncovers how categorization thinking operates with varied degrees of reductionism and consequently endorses fixed and stationary understandings of life and the world. The approach is incompatible with an idea of identity founded in categorizing ethnicity and nationality, common in migration studies. In retaining the senses of "uniqueness" and "mystery," as articulated by Levinas, my interlocutors' life-journeys reveal a complexity that is inadequately encompassed by a notion of identity.

A first issue to call attention to is the question of coherence. The complex rendition of the life-journeys in this ethnography questions the assumption of coherent identities by showing how contradictions and ambiguities are substantially embedded in the making of people's lives. The approach of life-journeys makes incongruity and inconsistency something integral to the experience of being-in-the-world with others. Furthermore, the complexity involved in the unfolding of the portrayed life-journeys contests the supposition of unity and completeness. Because it relies on modes of categorizations and coherence, identity in migration studies is a designation that does not encourage the consideration of "messy" or "scrappy" ways of existing. Furthermore, these studies frequently do not take into account different temporalities and the possibility of "unexpected" transformations, because of the influence exerted by the operation of generalization as an act of classification. Challenging the senses of coherence, unity, and completeness implicated in notions of identity often used in migration studies, the approach through the poetics of resonance and life-journeys suggests an alternative that considers contradiction, ambiguity, inconsistency, and incompleteness working elements in the making of ways of being and becoming. I consolidate this alternative via the idea of "immensity."

Rapport defines immensity as an "inventiveness free from normative and ideological constraints, a potentially limitless, expansion of being" (2003: 42). Such enlargement of being, possible when emphasis is not placed on single categories to define it, operates in terms of a "both/and" attitude, in which a person is able to live "a plurality of social worlds at any one time" and "the symbolic classifications and social structures of human worlds do not stand alone or uncontested or in clear and coherent relationship to one another" (Rapport 1997a: 671). The idea of immensity sustains this possibility of simultaneously preserving diverse and conflicting realms of subjectivity. Alongside it, another fundamental aspect composing the idea of immensity is the recognition of the "mystery" in each being, as Levinas (1987) conceived it, and the "stranger in ourselves," as Chambers (1994:6) described it. Only by admitting this ungraspable part in the constitution of any self can the inner character of a person be deemed open-ended and "acquire a form that is always contingent, in transit, without goal, without an end" (Chambers 1994: 25). Jackson (2013) argues that migrants' selves in anthropology should be "descriptions of human improvisation, experimentation, opportunism, and existential mobility, showing that individuals often struggle less with aligning their lives with given moral or legal norms than with finding ways of negotiating *the ethical space* between external constraints and personal imperatives" (2013: 203, my italics).

Returning to the life-journeys of this ethnography, Kitty, Helen, Mr. Kwon, Julieta, and Liu undertook very personal trajectories in São Paulo. Some of them struggled to be attached to a single national belonging, while others entertained multiple experiences of belonging or detached themselves from them. Although some of them relied on national-cum-ethnic categorizations, the incoherent and unstable experiences lived through their life-journeys made their trajectories vulnerable and incomplete. In trying not to be "multiple" in national terms, Mr. Kwon and Kitty were constantly overwhelmed by unexpected circumstances that defied the limited coherence of their categorical choice. In oscillating between national categories of affiliation, Julieta lived through the paradoxes of making sense of diverse standards at the same time. Helen in particular developed an awareness that categories of nationality were not sufficient to give expression to what she was, is, and will be; while Liu rejected being limited by any category of nationality that prevented her from achieving the good life. Each life-journey reveals the stakes of everyday life each of them had to endure and the capacities they engaged in order to cope with the challenges of their respective trajectories. In the instability and potentiality of their courses, Kitty's, Mr. Kwon's, Helen's, Julieta's, and Liu's immensities were unveiled.

In exploring these immensities, this experimental ethnography concurs with contemporary studies conceiving of subjectivity as "the ground for subjects to think through their circumstances and to feel through their contradictions" (Biehl et al. 2007: 14). The inner life of subjects is then considered an opportunity for "engaging with the complexity of people's lives and desires—their constraints, subjectivities, projects—in ever-changing social worlds" (Biehl and Locke 2010: 320). These studies then recognize "the indispensable moral and analytical value of the micro, the singular and partial" in ethnography, which "requires a different, more fine-grained, and humble logic than that of a generality subsuming all things into aggregates, repetitions, and models (Biehl and Locke 2017: xi).

Accompanying this elaboration of the notion of immensity, I will, in the next section, invoke observations about São Paulo as the urban space that vivify the existence of such social and subjective processes.

The Vanishing Point

SAINT-PAUL

J'adore cette ville
Saint-Paul est selon mon cœur
Ici nulle tradition
Aucun préjugé
Ni ancien ni moderne
Seuls comptent cet appétit furieux cette confiance ab-
    solue cet optimisme cette audace ce travail ce labeur
    cette spéculation qui font construire dix maisons
    par heure de tous styles ridicules grotesques beaux
    grands petits nord sud égyptien yankee cubiste
Sans autre préoccupation que de suivre les statistiques
    prévoir l'avenir le confort l'utilité la plus-value et
    d'attirer une grosse immigration
Tous les pays
Tous les peuples
J'aime ça
Le deux trois vieilles maisons portugaises qui restent
    son des faïences bleues[2]
                Blaise Cendrars, *Feuilles de Route*, 1924.

---

2.   French (my translation):

I love this city
St. Paul is in my heart
Here no tradition
No prejudice
Neither ancient nor modern
Only this furious appetite this absolute confidence this op-
    timism this audacity this work this labor this speculation
    that build ten houses per hour of all styles ridiculous gro-
    tesque beautiful large small north south Egyptian Yankee
    Cubist

The São Paulo which the poet and writer Blaise Cendrars honored in his verses—while enjoying the company of Brazilian intellectuals and modernist artists in the 1920s—is very different from the contemporary São Paulo of today. Yet, the fragmentary and jumbled portrait he sketched decades ago continues to be a poetic observation of a city that has challenged any definitive explanation. São Paulo is manifold and, possibly, the only incontestable statement one can assert is that it is an everchanging city. In paying attention to Kitty's, Mr. Kwon's, Helen's, Julieta's, and Liu's life-journeys, São Paulo was animated by their lives becoming intertwined with an urban space. No one lives a city in general, since it is not possible to be a general presence at all points at once. A city is made alive through the multiple and specific engagements its inhabitants are able to establish with it, sometimes in unexpected ways. The São Paulo that Kitty's and Mr. Kwon's life-journeys enlivened was a city of informal arrangements, of networks suffused of suspicion and mistrust; whereas for Helen's way of thinking it was a more malleable environment where she was able not to join Koreans family events and to commute to other neighborhoods to learn Portuguese. Regarding Julieta and Liu, even though they both held the same interest in giving birth in the city, they engaged São Paulo distinctly through diverse trajectories.

With no other concern than following the statistics, predicting the future comfort usefulness added value and attracting gross numbers of immigration.

All countries

All peoples

I like this

The two three old Portuguese houses that remain are of blue tiles.

For the former, São Paulo allowed her to merge activist beliefs and personal values by pursuing natural childbirth. For the latter, the city could not offer her and her family the good life, but could provide the necessary documents for them to accomplish it elsewhere. In this way, São Paulo as a city of "faces" cannot be expressed in absolute terms—it becomes multitudinous and disparate, as observed through Kitty's, Mr. Kwon's, Helen's, Julieta's, and Liu's life-journeys.

In the varied predicaments Kitty, Helen, Mr. Kwon, Julieta and Liu were entangled, uncertainty and instability intimately pervaded their trajectories in the city and beyond. As Simone (2005) argues these contexts of vulnerability are also opportunities for the creation of new urban sensibilities, whereby people are then impelled to open up their character and position to new possibilities. In this way, São Paulo might never be a resolved city, but, in its deficiency and incompleteness, it offers itself as potentiality (Simone 2016): potentiality to allow people from all walks of life and all parts of the globe to find their own ways in the city; and a potentiality to intermittently exceed lawfulness and become highly unstable. In rendering São Paulo through the singularity of varied life-journeys, the roughness and incongruities of the city becomes apparent; this provides a more nuanced picture in which the precarious and the contingent play a role in the constitution of urban processes.

Simultaneously, we could approach São Paulo as a city ingrained with and in migrants' trajectories as shown by the way it became a significant component in the transformation of Kitty's, Helen's, Mr. Kwon's, Julieta's and Liu's lives and selves. On that account, the ethnographic work tailored here unfolded scenarios of a city in constant movement and transformation, as enacted by each life-journey, revealing São Paulo as an existential experience through people's life-journeys. By offering a kaleidoscopic vision, these journeys expose São Paulo as a complex urban form which refuses to be grasped as a whole, as Cendrars poetically intuited. Such a proposition is advanced by Ananya Roy (2011) through the concept of "vanishing point." Borrowing this from Chantal Mouffe, Roy encourages us to consider cities like São Paulo as vanishing points, "something to which we must constantly refer, but that which can never be reached" (Roy 2011: 235); in our approach, every life-journey provides a unique portrayal of the city. The immensity of Kitty's, Helen's, Mr. Kwon's, Julieta's and Liu's lives testify to the immensity of São Paulo as an urban space.

And then . . .

Abu-Lughod, proposing new textual strategies to write "against culture," claims that "ethnographies of the particular" are "instruments of tactical humanism" (1991: 137). In this experimental ethnography, the particular was pushed to its extreme as an alternative to understand the human through complexities outside processes of generalization, simplification and reductionism. In taking seriously the responsibility to "do justice" to the "mystery" I found in people, places, and situations, a new horizon of analysis emerged. This mystery imbued the subtle aspects of the lives of the international mobile actors I followed, especially in those fleeting moments of inarticulacy and hesitation that revealed to me how life could be an unstable and uncertain endeavor. I found in Levinas an inspirational body of work that allowed me to explore the possibility of considering mystery an integral part of a research exploration. Levinas offered me a way to compose a feasible ethnographic experiment that held mystery as a core concern through the notion of the Other's "uniqueness." Upon this theoretical reference, and resisting "totalization," as Levinas calls the expressions of extreme systematization in thought, the concept of "uniqueness" was transmuted ethnographically into the idea of the "life-journey." By unfolding the experiences of Mr. Kwon, Kitty, Julieta, Helen and Liu through the notion of life-journey, the singularity of their existences was enlivened.

Their life-journeys indicated in varied ways how a life, lived as a series of events occurring in particular moments and places, is susceptible to all sorts of incongruities and contrarieties. In order to acknowledge such "imponderabilia of actual life" as part of the process of making life, I crafted a "poetics of resonance" to put them into relief by "rendering delirious that interior voice that it is the voice of the other in us" (Spivak 1988: 104), as Spivak underlines Derrida's insight. Mystery was then methodologically incorporated by a cosmopolitan attitude (Rapport 2012a) that not only does not deem cultural or social categorizations as key references for a research project, but believes that we as humans share the capacity to put ourselves in the place of the other, though one will never get to be the other. Imagination was, in this way tailored to reconcile the ethical breach between research and the unsurmountable enigma of every subject, working as a textual attendance to those inchoate and vulnerable moments I sensed in the lives of the research participants I had the opportunity to follow. Thus, the poetics of resonance here signals the limitations of any research approach in knowing everything about a subject, and indicates how the fragility of those lives, disturbed by specific occurrences, disrupted notions of ethnicity, nationality, kinship, or citizenship.

It is my hope that, after appreciating the singular lives portrayed in this ethnography, I might persuade the reader that it is worth attempting such an alternative way of doing anthropology in order to reach a different appreciation of the human in the world. Some may say that there is nothing remarkable in the life-journeys vivified here, as they are trivial and ordinary. But this ethnographic experiment is an attempt to show that every life is a unique risk and adventure that worth recognizing. This appreciation offered some insights concerning migration studies. In all the life-journeys portrayed, senses of belonging were uniquely shaped, leading to very different trajectories in São Paulo. Mr. Kwon and Kitty strived to keep the unity of their existences through ethnicity-cum-nationality. Mr. Kwon recurrently stated his affiliation as Korean, while Kitty discreetly asserted her belonging as Paraguayan. Both of them preferred to operate within the fixity of only one national reference, while Julieta moved around multiple senses of belonging. Whereas the life-journeys of Julieta connected senses of being Bolivian, with those of being an activist, a mother and a devotee—finding a wider range of possibilities within these references—Helen's life-journey experimented with new ways of being beyond the standards of being Korean. Distinctively, Liu disengaged from her original nationality by manipulating bureaucratic procedures of citizenship worldwide to reach her ideal of a good life. These life-processes, thus, reflected the different manners in which each life-journey configured senses of self in immensity. In holding themselves up to national-cum-ethnic references of belonging, Mr. Kwon, Kitty, and Julieta anchored their life-journeys to personal, but tensioned, notions of nationality. Whereas Mr. Kwon and Kitty grappled with retaining the unity of these identities, Julieta alternated between the references of being Bolivian and other sorts of position, affirming to be a Bolivian with diverse experiences in Brazil. Alternatively, in generating their own justification for living beyond the categories of national-cum-ethnic categorizations, Helen and Liu afforded the opportunity to produce an open-ended sense of self through the potentialities of their immensity, highlighting the fact that life is a process that continuously extends into the future (Dalsgaard and Frederiksen 2013).

In the context of migration studies, this ethnographic experiment found that ethnicity and nationality are not the only references constituting migrants' lives. They can be significant, as it was evidenced in the lives of Kitty, Helen, Mr. Kwon, Julieta, but ethnicity and nationality were not sufficient references in themselves. In eschewing an approach to the lives of international migrants living in São Paulo through preordained social categorizations, the life-journeys of the research participants involved were emphasized to show that norms or categories of ethnicity, nationality, kinship, or citizenship become just another aspect in lives full of uncertainty, risk, and tribulations. In following their experiences as life-journeys, these categories have been shown to be contradictorily lived, as they were constantly questioned by a new event in their trajectories. Furthermore, each life-journey expressed a very singular incarnation of the capacity each person possessed to enliven a life, allowing anthropology to approach the human as ethnographic densities.

In questioning "categorisation thinking" in migration studies, a new sense of complexity emerged, following Levinas's notions of "uniqueness" and "mystery." From this new sense of complexity, the idea of multiplicity could be reconfigured. This allowed for *thinking of identities as "immensities": a denomination for subjectivities that can contain contradictions and ambiguities in themselves, holding capacities to deal with the unknown and unexpected of the world, therefore, being open-ended and incomplete.* Concomitantly, São Paulo, as a city accommodating such immensities, became a kaleidoscopic urban space, opened to every trajectory that ventured to affect the city and be affected by it. Through the different life-journeys developed in São Paulo and beyond, distinct accounts of the city were enacted.

This ethnographic experiment has refused to reduce human lives to general schemes in which one cannot identify faces anymore. The efforts applied here manifest the attempt to create an anthropology that is able to acknowledge the richness of what is to live a life through thick and thin, recognizing the meaning of what is to be singular in a world lived as movement and uncertainty.

References

Abu-Lughod, Lila. 1991. "Writing Against Culture." In *Recapturing Anthropology: Working in the Present*. Edited by Richard Fox, 137–62. Santa Fe: School of American Research Press.

Allison, Anne. 2013. *Precarious Japan*. Durham: Duke University Press.

Amit, Vered. 2011. " 'Before I Settle Down': Youth Travel and Enduring Life Course Paradigms." *Anthropologica* 53 (1): 79–88.

Amit-Talai, Vered. 1995. "Anthropology, Multiculturalism and the Concept of Culture." *Folk* 37: 135–44.

Baeninger, Rosana. 2012. *Fases e Faces da Migração em São Paulo*. Campinas: Nepo/Unicamp.

Baeninger, Rosana and Peres, Roberta G. 2011. "Refugiados Africanos em São Paulo: Espaços da Migração." *Revista Internacional de Língua Portuguesa* 24: 97–112.

Bakhtin, Mikhail. 1981. *The Dialogic Imagination: Four Essays*. Edited by Michael Holquist. Translated by Caryl Emerson and Michael Holquist. Austin: University of Texas Press.

163

Basch, Linda, Nina Glick Schiller, and Cristina Szanton Blanc. 1994. *Nations Unbound: Transnational Projects, Postcolonial Predicaments, and Deterritorialized Nation-States*. Basel: Gordon and Breach Science.

Bauman, Gerd. 1996. *Contesting Culture: Discourses of Identity in Multi-ethnic London*. Cambridge: Cambridge University Press.

Bauman, Gerd, and Thijl Sunier. 1995. *Post-migration Ethnicity: De-essentializing Cohesion, Commitments, and Comparison*. Amsterdam: Het Spinhuis Publishers.

Beck, Ulrich. 1992. *Risk Society: Towards a New Modernity*. London: Sage.

———. 2006. *The Cosmopolitan Vision*. Cambridge: Polity Press.

———. 2009. "Critical Theory of World Risk Society: A Cosmopolitan Vision." *Constellations* 16 (1): 3–22.

Behar, Ruth. 1993. *Translated Woman: Crossing the Border with Esperanza's Story*. Boston: Beacon Press.

Bergson, Henri. 1959a [1889]. "Essai sur les Données Immédiates de la Conscience." In *Ouvres*, 3–157. Paris: Presses Universitaires de France.

———. 1959b [1907]. "L'évolution Créative." In *Ouvres*, 487–811. Paris: Presses Universitaires de France.

Berthomé, François, Julien Bonhomme, and Grégory Delaplace. 2012. "Cultivating Uncertainty." *HAU: Journal of Ethnographic Theory* 2 (2): 129–37.

Bhachu, Parminder. 1985. *Twice Migrants: East African Sikh Settlers in Britain*. London: Tavistock.

Biehl, João, Byron Good, and Arthur Kleiman. 2007. "Introduction: Rethinking subjectivity." In *Subjectivity: Ethnographic Investigations*, 1–24. Berkeley: University of California Press.

Biehl, João, and Peter Locke. 2010. "Deleuze and the Anthropology of Becoming." *Current Anthropology* 51 (3): 317–51.

Biehl, João, and Peter Locke. 2017. "Foreword." In *Unfinished: The Anthropology of Becoming*. Edited by Biehl, João, and Peter Locke, i–xiii. Durham: Duke University Press.

Bonduki, Nabil. and Rolnik, Raquel. 1979. *Periferia: Ocupação do Espaço e Reprodução da Força de Trabalho*. São Paulo: Faculdade de Arquitetura e Urbanismo/ Fundação para a Pesquisa Ambiental.

Brettell, Caroline. 2018 "Conceptualizing Migration and Mobility in Anthropology: An Historical Analysis." *Transitions: Journal of Transient Migration*, 2 (1): 7-25.

Butler, Judith. 2004. *Precarious Life: The Powers of Mourning and Violence*. London: Verso.

——. 2010. *Frames of War: When is Life Grievable?* London: Verso.

Caldeira, Teresa. 1984. *A Política dos Outros: o Cotidiano dos Moradores e da Periferia e o que Pensam do Poder e dos Poderosos*. São Paulo: Brasiliense.

——. 2000. *City of Walls:Crime, Segregation, and Citizenship in São Paulo*. Berkeley: University of California Press.

Cardoso, Ruth. 1986. "Aventuras de Antropólogos em Campo ou Como Escapar das Armadilhas do Método." In *A Aventura Antropológica*. Edited by Ruth Cardoso, 95-106. São Paulo: Editora Paz e Terra.

Castles, Stephen, Hein de Haas, and Mark J. Miller. 2014. *The Age of Migration: International Population Movements in the Modern World*. Hampshire: Palgrave Macmillan.

Cendrars, Blaise. 1987 [1924]. "Saint Paul." In *Du Monde Entire au Coeur du Monde*, 215. Paris: Denoël.

Chambers, Iain. 1994. *Migrancy, Culture, Identity*. London and New York: Routledge.

Chi, Jung Yun. 2016a. *O Bom Retiro dos Coreanos: Descrição de um Enclave Étnico*. Master's diss., Faculdade de Arquitetura e Urbanismo, Universidade de São Paulo, São Paulo.

———. 2016b. "Imigrantes Coreanos na Formação do Pólo Atacadista de Moda Feminina de Pronta-entrega no Bairro do Bom Retiro, São Paulo." In *Pós, Revista do Programa de Pós Graduação em Arquitetura e Urbanismo da FAU-USP*, 23 (41): 90–107.

Choi, Keum Joa. 1991. *Além do Arco-íris: a Imigração Coreana no Brasil*. Master's Diss., Faculdade de Filosofia, Letras e Ciências Humanas, Universidade de São Paulo, São Paulo.

———. 2009. "The Characteristics and Prospect of the Korean community in Brazil in the Era of Neoliberalism." *Korean Society of Portuguese-Brazilian Studies* 6 (2): 205–53.

Clifford, James. 1986. "Introduction: Partial Truths." in *Writing Culture: The Poetics and Politics of Ethnography*. Edited by James Clifford and George Marcus, 1–27. Berkeley: University of California Press.

Cohen, Anthony. 1996. "Personal Nationalism: A Scottish View of Some Rites, Rights, and Wrongs." *American Ethnologist* 23 (4): 802–15.

Cohen, Anthony, and Nigel Rapport. 1995. "Introduction: Consciousness in Anthropology." In *Questions of Consciousness*. Edited by Anthony Cohen and Nigel Rapport, 1–20. London: Routledge.

Comin, Alvaro. 2011. "Cidades-Regiões ou Hiperconcentração do Desenvolvimento? O Debate Visto do Sul." In *São Paulo: Novos Percursos e Atores*. Edited by Lúcio

Kowarick and Eduardo Marques, 157–177. São Paulo: Editora 34.

Cooper, Elizabeth, and David Pratten. 2015. "Ethnographies of Uncertainty in Africa: An Introduction." In *Ethnographies of Uncertainty in Africa*. Edited by Elizabeth Cooper and David Pratten, 1–16. Hampshire: Palgrave Macmillan.

Côrtes, Tiago R. 2014. "Paraguaios em São Paulo: Uma História e um Retrato." *Travessia*, 27 (74): 13–36.

Côrtes, Tiago R. and Silva, Carlos F. 2014. "Migrantes na Costura em São Paulo: Paraguaios, Bolivianos e Brasileiros na Indústria de Confecções." *Travessia*, 27 (74): 37–58.

Cresswell, Tim. 2006. *On the Move: Mobility in the Modern Western World*. New York: Routledge.

Dalsgaard, Anne L, and Martin D Frederiksen. 2013. "Out of Conclusion: On Recurrence and Open-endedness in Life and Analysis." *Social Analysis*, 57(1): 50-63.

——. 2014. "Introduction: Time Objectified" In *Ethnographies of Youth and Temporality: Time Objectified*. Edited by Anne L. Dalsgard, Martin Frederiksen, Susanne Hojlund, Lotte Meinert, and Michael G. Flaherty, p. 1–22. Philadelphia: Temple University Press.

Davis, Mike. 2006. *Planet of Slums*. London: Verso.

De Oliveira, Antonio T. R. 2019. "A Migração Venezuelana no Brasil: Crise Humanitária, Desinformação e os Aspectos Normativos." *Revista de Estudos e Pesquisas sobre as Américas* 13(1), 219–244.

De Oliveira, Márcio. 2018. "A Sociologia da Imigração no Brasil Entre as Décadas de 1940 e 1970." *Sociologias* 20 (49): 198–228.

Dewey, J. 1980 [1934]. *Art as Experience*. New York: The Berkley Publishing Group.

——. 2008 [1925]. "Experience and Nature." In *John Dewey: The Later Works, 1925–1953*, Volume 1, 3–327. Carbondale: Southern Illinois University Press.

Dezem, Rogério. 2005. *Matizes do "Amarelo": A Gênese dos Discursos Sobre os Orientais no Brasil (1878-1908)*. São Paulo: Associação Editorial Humanitas.

Dilthey, Wilhelm. 1985 [1887]. *Poetry and Experience*. Princeton, NJ: Princeton University Press.

——. 1989 [1883]. *Introduction to the Human Sciences*. Princeton, NJ: Princeton University Press.

——. 2002 [1910]. *The Formation of the Historical World in Human Sciences*. Princeton, NJ: Princeton University Press.

Dilthey, Wilhelm, and Fredric Jameson. 1972. "The Rise of Hermeneutics." *New Literary History* 3 (2): 229–44.

Dumont, Louis. 1986. *Essays on Individualism: Modern Ideology in Anthropological Perspective*. Chicago: University of Chicago Press.

Durkheim, Émile. 1995 [1902]. *Elementary Forms Of The Religious Life*. Translated By Karen E. Fields. New York, NY: Free Press.

——. 2014 [1893]. *The Division of Labor in Society*. Edited and Translated by Steven Lukes. New York, NY: Free Press.

Elias, Norbert. 1993. *Mozart: Portrait of a Genius*. Cambridge, MA: Polity.

Erdal, Marta Bivand, and Ceri Oeppen. 2018. "Forced to Leave? The Discursive and Analytical Significance of Describing Migration as Forced and Voluntary." *Journal of Ethnic and Migration Studies* 44 (6): 981–998.

Eriksen, Thomas. 2007. "Complexity in Social and Cultural Integration: Some Analytical Dimensions." *Ethnic and Racial Studies* 30 (6): 1055–69.

——. 2010. *Ethnicity and Nationalism: Anthropological Perspectives*. London: Pluto Press.

Ermarth, Michael. 1978. *Wilhelm Dilthey: Critique of Historical Reason*. Chicago: University of Chicago Press.

Feldman-Bianco, Bela. 2001. "Portuguese in Brazil, Brazilians in Portugal: Constructions of Sameness and Difference." *Identities: Global Studies in Culture and Power* 8 (4): 607–650.

Freire da Silva, Carlos. 2014. *Das Calçadas às Galerias: Mercados Populares do Centro de São Paulo*. Doctoral diss., Department of Sociology, University of São Paulo, São Paulo.

——. 2018. "Conexões Brasil-China: a Migração Chinesa no Centro de São Paulo." *Cadernos Metropolitanos* 20 (41): 223–243.

Frúgoli, Heitor. 2000. *Centralidade em São Paulo: Trajetórias, Conflitos e Negociações na Metrópole*. São Paulo: Edusp.

Frúgoli, Heitor and Sklair, Jessica. 2009. "O Bairro da Luz em São Paulo: Questões Antropológicas sobre o Fenômeno da Gentrification." *Cuadernos de Antropologia Social*, 30: 119–136.

Frúgoli, Heitor and Spaggiari, Enrico. 2010. "Da 'Cracolândia' aos Nóias: Percursos Etnográficos no Bairro da Luz." *Ponto Urbe*, 4 (6),

Glick Schiller, Nina and Salazar, Noel. 2013. "Regimes of Mobility Across the Globe." *Journal of Ethnic and Migration Studies*, 39 (2): 183-200.

Guo, Bingqiang. 2005. *Registro Geral dos Imigrantes Chineses de Qingtian no Brasil (1910-1994)*. Qingtian: China.

Hannerz, Ulf. 1996. *Transnational Connections*. London: Routledge.

Haraway, Donna. 1991. *Simians, Cyborgs, and Women: The Reinvention of Nature.* New York: Routledge.

Harris, Mark, and Nigel Rapport. 2015. *Reflections on Imagination: Human Capacity and Ethnographic Method.* Farnham and Burlington: Ashgate.

Harvey, David. 1990. *The Condition of Postmodernity: An Enquiry into the Origins of Cultural Change.* Oxford: Blackwell.

—. 2012. *Rebel Cities: From the Right to the City to the Urban Revolution.* London: Verso.

Hastrup, Kristin. 1995. "The Inarticulate mind: The place of Awareness in Social Action." In *Questions of Consciousness.* Edited by Anthony P. Cohen and Nigel Rapport, 181–97. London: Routledge.

Heidegger, Martin. 2010 [1953]. *Being and Time.* Translated by Joan Stambaugh. New York: State University of New York Press.

Hollan, Douglas. 2008. "Being There: On the Imaginative Aspects of Understanding Others and Being Understood." *Ethos* 36: 475–89.

Holston, James. 2009. "Insurgent Citizenship in an Era of Global Urban Peripheries." *City & Society* 21, (2) 245–67.

Hua-Sheng, Hsia. 2008. "Modelos de Financiamento Baseados em Relações Pessoais: Experiência de Empreendedores Chineses no Brasil." *Revista de Administração Contemporânea.* 12 (3): 741–761.

Hyndman, Jennifer. 2000. *Managing Displacement: Refugees and the Politics of Humanitarianism.* Minneapolis: University of Minnesota Press.

Jackson, Michael. 2005. *Existential Anthropology.* New York: Berghahn Books.

——. 2013. *The Wherewithal of Life: Ethics, Migration, and the Question of Well-Being*. Berkeley: University of California Press.

Jankowiak, William. 2008. "Well Being, Cultural Pathology, and Personal Rejuvenation in a Chinese City: 1981-2005." In *Pursuits of Happiness: Well Being in Anthropological Perspective*. Edited by Gordon Mathews and Carolina Izquierdo, 147–166. Oxford: Berghahn Publishers.

Kim, Chong-Sup, and Eunsuk Lee. 2016. "Growth and Migration to a Third Country: The Case of Korean Migrants in Latin America." *Journal of International and Area Studies* 23 (2): 77–87.

Khosravi, Shahram. 2017. *Precarious Lives: Waiting and Hope in Iran*. Philadelphia: University of Pennsylvania Press.

Kowarick, Lúcio. 2009. *Viver em Risco: Sobre a Vulnerabilidade Socioeconômica e Civil*. São Paulo: Editora 34.

Lash, Scott, and John Urry. 1988. *The end of Organized Capitalism*. Gerrards Cross: Polity Press.

——. 1994. *Economies of Signs and Space*. London: Sage.

Law, John. 2004. *After Method: Mess in Social Science Research*. New York: Routledge.

Lesser, Jeffrey. 1999. *Negotiating National Identity: Immigrants, Minorities, and the Struggle for Ethnicity in Brazil*. Durham, NC: Duke University Press.

Levinas, Emmanuel. 1967. *Totality and Infinity*. Translated by Alphonso Lingis. Pittsburgh: Duquesne University Press.

——. 1987. *Time and the Other*. Translated by Richard A. Cohen. Pittsburgh: Duquesne University Press.

———. 1989. "Ethics as first philosophy." In *The Levinas Reader*. Edited by Seán Hand, 75–87. Oxford: Basil Blackwell.

———. 1998. *Entre Nous: On Thinking-of-the-Other*. Translated by Michael B. Smith and Barbara Harshav, 162–68. London: Continuum.

Levitt, Peggy, and Nina Glick Schiller. 2004. "Conceptualizing Simultaneity: A Transnational Social Field Perspective on Society." *The International Migration Review* 38 (3): 1002–39.

Lubkemann, Stephen. 2008. *Culture in Chaos: An Anthropology of the Social Condition in War*. Chicago: The University of Chicago Press.

Magnani, José. 1998. *Festa no Pedaço: Cultura Popular e Lazer na Cidade*. São Paulo: Editora Unesp/Editora Hucitec.

Maldonado, Oscar. 2016. "A Invisibilidade dos Paraguaios em São Paulo" In *Migração, Trabalho e Cidadania: Patrimônios Culturais do Brasil*. Edited by Dirceu Cutti, Dulce Maria T. Baptista, José Carlos Pereira, Lucia Maria M. Bógus, 151–171. São Paulo: EDUC.

Malinowski, Bronislaw. 1932. *Argonauts of the Western Pacific*. London: George Routledge and Sons.

Margolis, Maxine L. 2013. *Goodbye, Brazil: Emigrantes Brasileiros no Mundo*. São Paulo: Contexto.

Maricato, Ermínia. 1999. "Metrópole de São Paulo, Entre o Arcaico e a Pós-modernidade" In *Metrópole e Globalização*. São Paulo: Cedesp.

Monteiro, Rafael and Bastos, Sênia. 2011. "Imigração Coreana: A Questão da Reemigração e do Retorno." *Revista do Migrante*. 69: 47-55.

Nussbaum, Martha. 1995. "Human Capabilities, Female Human Beings." In *Women, Culture, and Development:*

A Study of Human Capabilities. Edited by Martha Nussbaum and Jonathan Glover, 62–105. Oxford: Oxford University Press. E-book.

Ong, Aihwa. 1999. *Flexible Citizenship: The Cultural Logics of Transnationality.* Durham: Duke University Press.

Organização Internacional para as Migrações. 2019. *Perfil 2019 da Cidade de São Paulo: Indicadores da Governança Migratória Local (MGI).* Geneva: IOM

Pardue, Derek. 2010. "Making Territorial Claims: Brazilian Hip Hop and the Socio-Geographical Dynamics of Periferia." *City & Society* 22 (1): 48–71.

Park, Kyeyoung. 1999. " 'I am Floating in the Air:' Creation of a Korean Transnational Space among Korean-Latino American Remigrants.' *Positions* 7(3): 667–69.

——. 2014. "A Rhizomatic Diaspora: Transnational Passage and The Sense of Place Among Koreans In Latin America" In *Urban Anthropology and Studies of Cultural Systems and World Economic Development,* 43 (4): 481–517.

Patarra, Neide L. and Fernandes, Duval. 2011. "Brasil: País de Imigração?" *Revista Internacional de Língua Portuguesa* 24: 65–96.

Pinheiro-Machado, Rosana. 2008. "China-Paraguai-Brasil: Uma Rota para Pensar a Economia Informal." *Revista Brasileira de Ciências Sociais,* 23, (67): 117–133.

Pink, Sara, Yoko Akama, and Shanti Sumartojo. 2018. *Uncertainty and Possibility: New Approaches To Future-Making in Design Anthropology.* London: Bloomsbury.

Profit, Alena. 2014. "A Imigração Paraguaia Contemporânea: Elementos para sua Compreensão." *Revista Interdisciplinar sobre Mobilidade Humana,* 22 (43): 281–84.

Ramos, Jair de Souza. 1996. "Dos Males Que vêm Com o Sangue: As Representações Raciais e a Categoria do Imigrante Indesejável nas Concepções Sobre a Imigração da Década de 20." In *Raça, Ciência e Sociedade*. Edited by Marcos Chor Maio and Ricardo Ventura Santos, 59–82. Rio de Janeiro: Fio Cruz.

Rapport, Nigel. 1993. *Diverse World-views in an English Village*. Edinburgh: Edinburgh University Press.

——. 1997a. "The 'Contrarieties' of Israel: An Essay on the Cognitive Importance and the Creative Promise of Both/And." *Journal of the Royal Anthropological Institute* 3 (4): 653–72.

——. 1997b. *Transcendent individual: Towards a Literary and Liberal Anthropology*, 30–42. London and New York: Routledge.

——. 2003. *I Am Dynamite: An Alternative Anthropology of Power*. London: Routledge.

——. 2009. "The 'Human' as the Issue of Anthropology" *Anthropologica* 51: 109–14.

——. 2010. "Human Capacity as an Exceeding, a Going Beyond." In *Human Nature as Capacity: Transcending Discourse and Classification*. Edited by Nigel Rapport, 1–28. New York and Oxford: Berghahn Books.

——. 2012a. *Anyone: The Cosmopolitan Subject of Anthropology*. New York: Berghahn.

——. 2012b. " 'Tensile Nationality': National Identity as an Everyday Way of Being in a Scottish Hospital." *Anthropology in Action* 19 (1): 60–73.

——. 2015. "Anthropology through Levinas: Knowing the Uniqueness of Ego and the Mystery of Otherness." *Current Anthropology* 56 (2): 256–76.

Rapport, Nigel, and Andrew Dawson. 1994. *Migrants of Identity: Perceptions of Home in a World of Movement.* Oxford: Berg.

Rapport, Nigel, and Ron Stade. 2007. "A Cosmopolitan Turn—or Return?" *Social Anthropology* 15 (2): 223–35.

Rodríguez, Encarnación Gutiérrez. 2018. "Conceptualizing the Coloniality of Migration: On European Settler Colonialism-Migration, Racism, and Migration Policies". In *Migration: Changing Concepts, Critical Approaches*. Edited by Doris Bachmann-Medick and Jens Kugele, 193-210. Berlin: De Gruyter.

Rolnik, Raquel. 1999. "Territorial Exclusion and Violence: The Case of São Paulo, Brazil." Comparative Urban Studies Occasional Papers Series, 26. Washington, D.C.: Woodrow Wilson International Center for Scholars. https://pdf.usaid.gov/pdf_docs/Pnacl303.pdf

Rosaldo, Renato. 1989. *Culture and Truth: The Remaking of Social Analysis*, ix–xx. Boston: Beacon Press.

Roy, Ananya. 2011. "Slumdog Cities: Rethinking Subaltern Urbanism." *International Journal of Urban and Regional Research* 35 (2): 223–238.

Rui, Taniele. 2014. *Nas Tramas do Crack: Etnografia da Abjeção*. São Paulo: Terceiro Nome.

Sajjad, Tazreena. 2018. "What's in a Name? 'Refugees', 'Migrants' and the Politics of Labelling." *Class & Race* 60 (2): 40–62.

Sampaio, Maria R. 2011. "Os Coreanos no Bom Retiro." In *São Paulo, os Estrangeiros e a Construção das Cidades*. Edited by Ana Lanna, Fernanda Peixoto, Joao de Lima, and Maria Sampaio, 89–115. São Paulo: Alameda.

Sayad, Abdelmalek. 2006. "Le Retour: Élément Constitutif de la Condition de l'Immigré." In *L'immigration ou les Paradoxes de l'Altérité: L'illusion du Provisoire*, 131–192. Paris: Éditions Raisons d'Agir.

Schwarcz, Lilia M. 1993. *O Espetáculo das Raças*. São Paulo: Companhia das letras.

Seyferth, Giralda. 1996. "Construindo a Nação: Hierarquias Raciais e o Papel do Racismo na Política de Imigração e Colonização." In *Raça, Ciência e Sociedade*. Edited by Marcos Chor Maio and Ricardo Ventura Santos, 41–58. Rio de Janeiro: Fiocruz.

Sheller, Mimi and Urry, John. 2006. "The New Mobilities Paradigm." *Environment and Planning A: Economy and Space*, 38(2), 207–226.

Shostak, Marjorie. 1983. *Nisa: The Life and Words of a !Kung woman*. New York: Vintage Books.

Silva, João Carlos Jarochinski, Lucia Maria Machado Bógus and Stéfanie Angélica Gimenez. 2017. "Os Fluxos Migratórios Mistos e os Entraves à Proteção aos Refugiados." *Revista Brasileira de Estudos Populacionais* 34 (1): 15–30.

Silva, Sidney A. 1997. *Costurando Sonhos: Trajetória de um Grupo de Imigrantes Bolivianos que Trabalham no Ramo Da Costura em São Paulo*. São Paulo: Paulinas.

Silva, Sidney S., and Mello, Heloisa A. 2018. "Imigrantes Bolivianos no Brasil: um Reflexo da Pluralidade Cultural e Linguística Boliviana em São Paulo." *Revista de Estudos Literários da UEMS* 1 (18): 125–151.

Simmel, Georg. 1971 [1911]. "The Adventure." In *On Individuality and Social Forms*. Edited by Donald Levine, 187–98. Chicago: University of Chicago Press.

Simone, AbdouMaliq. 2005. "Urban Circulation and the Everyday Politics of African Urban Youth: The Case of Douala, Cameroon." *International Journal of Urban and Regional Research* 29 (3): 516–32.

——. 2016. "City of Potentialities: An Introduction." *Theory, Culture & Society* 33 (7– 8): 5–29.

Skidmore, Thomas E. 1993. *Black into White: Race and Nationality in Brazilian Thought*. Durham: Duke University Press.

Souchaud, Sylvain. 2011. "A Visão do Paraguai no Brasil." *Contexto Internacional*, 33(1), 131–153.

——. 2012. "A Confecção: Nicho Étnico ou Nicho Econômico Para Imigração Latino-Americana Em São Paulo?" In *Imigração Boliviana no Brasil*. Edited by Rosana Baeninger, 75–92. Campinas: Nepo/Unicamp: Fapesp: CNPq: UNFPA.

Spivak, Gayatri. 1988. "Can the Subaltern Speak?" In *Marxism and the Interpretation of Culture*. Edited by Cary Nelson and Lawrence Grossberg, 271–313. Urbana, IL: University of Illinois Press.

Standing, Guy. 2011. *The Precariat: The New Dangerous Class*. London: Bloomsbury Academic.

Stenberg, Josh. 2012. "The Chinese of São Paulo: A Case Study. Journal of Chinese Overseas." *Singapura* 8 (1): 105–122.

Taniguti, Gustavo. 2018. "O Imigrante Segundo as Ciências Sociais Brasileiras, 1940-1960." *Sociologias* 20 (49): 142–196.

Thiollet, Hélène. 2010. "Migrations et Relations Internationales." *Transcontinentales* [online] 8/9. https://journals.openedition.org/transcontinentales/787?gathStatIcon=true&lang=en

Thrift, Neil. 2008. *Non-Representational Theory: Space, Politics, Affect*. London and New York: Routledge.

Throop, Jason. 2002. "Experience, Coherence, and Culture: The Significance of Dilthey's 'Descriptive Psychology' for the Anthropology of Consciousness." *Anthropology of Consciousness* 13 (1): 2–26.

———. 2010. "Latitudes of Loss: On the Vicissitudes of Empathy." *American Ethnologist* 37: 771–82.

To, James. 2009. *Hand-In-Hand, Heart-To-Heart: Qiaowu and the Overseas Chinese.* Doctoral diss., University of Canterbury, New Zealand.

Toji, Simone. 2023. "On Catalina's Silence and the Things About Her I Still Do Not Know How to Say." In *The Entanglements of Ethnographic Fieldwork in a Violent World.* Edited by Nerina Weiss, Erella Grassiane and Linda Green, 114-121. Oxton, OX, and New York, NY: Routledge.

Truzzi, Oswaldo. 2001. "Etnias em Convívio: O Bairro do Bom Retiro em São Paulo." *Estudos Históricos* 27: 143–66.

———. 2008. "Redes em Processos Migratórios." *Tempo Social* 20 (1): 199–218.

Tsing, Anna. 2005. *Friction: An Ethnography of Global Connection.* Princeton, NJ and Oxford: Princeton University Press.

———. 2015. *The Mushroom at the End of the World: On the Possibility of Life in Capitalist Ruins.* Princeton, NJ: Princeton University Press.

Turner, Simon. 2015. "'We Wait for Miracles': Ideas of Hope and Future among Clandestine Burundian Refugees in Nairobi." In *Ethnographies of Uncertainty in Africa.* Edited by Elizabeth Cooper and David Pratten, 173–192. Hampshire and New York: Palgrave Macmillan.

Tyler, Stephen. 1986. "Postmodern Ethnography: From Document of the Occult to Occult Document." In *Writing Culture: The Poetics and Politics of Ethnography.* Edited by James Clifford and George Marcus, 122–39. Berkeley: University of California Press.

——.1987. *The Unspeakable: Discourse, Dialogue, and Rhetoric in the Postmodern World.* Madison, WI: University of Wisconsin Press.

United Nations Human Settlements Programme (UN-HABITAT). 2010. *São Paulo: A Tale of Two Cities.* Nairobi: UN HABITAT Office.

Urry, John. 2007. *Mobilities.* Cambridge: Polity Press.

Vaninni, Philip. 2015a. "Enlivening Ethnography through the Irrealist Mood in Search of a More-than-Representational Style." In *Non-Representational Methodologies: Re-Envisioning Research*, 112–29. New York: Routledge.

——. 2015b. "Non-representational Ethnography: New Ways of Animating Lifeworld." *Cultural Geographies* 22 (2): 317–27.

Verás, Daniel. 2008. *As Diásporas Chinesas e o Brasil: A Comunidade Sino-Brasileira em São Paulo.* Doctoral Diss., Pontifícia Universidade Católica de São Paulo, São Paulo.

Vertovec, Steven. 2010. *Anthropology of Migration and Multiculturalism.* London: Routledge.

Wikan, Unni. 2012. "Beyond the Words: The Power of Resonance." In *Resonance: Beyond the Word*s. Edited by Unni Wikan, 51–80. Chicago, IL and London: University of Chicago Press.

Zetter, Roger. 1991. "Labelling Refugees: Forming and Transforming a Bureaucratic Identity." *Journal of Refugee Studies* 4 (1): 39 – 62.

——. 2007. "More Labels, Fewer Refugees: Remaking the Refugee Label in an Era of Globalization." *Journal of Refugee Studies* 20 (2): 172 – 192.